KU-304-686

CARIBBEAN ISLANDS

JPMGUIDES

sun-drenched beaches

CONTENTS

water sports

the Caribbean beat

gone fishing

THIS WAY THE CARIBBEAN

The Caribbean islands laze in the sun, stretching across the ocean between North and South America. In the west, the Greater Antilles—Cuba, Jamaica, Hispaniola (divided between the Dominican Republic and Haiti), Puerto Rico—still bear the mark of the conquistadors. To the east, the four dozen Lesser Antilles, thrust from the depths in volcanic upheaval millions of years ago, form a rainbow arching from north to south, swept by the trade winds.

Specks of emerald set in a turquoise sea, beaches of fine white or golden sand fringed by shady palms swaying gently in the breeze, a colourful, luxuriant vegetation—the islands provide the perfect answer to our longing for escape, for peace and serenity and eternal sunshine.

But history was not kind to these islands. Behind the word "Caribbean" ring the echoes of a tumultuous past. Fabulous myths of Indian tribes and cannibals mingle with disappointed hopes of an Eldorado or a Fountain of Youth. Pirates and buccaneers ruled the waves. The Spaniards came and conquered, soon to be supplanted by the English and their bitter rivals, the French. Then Dutch, the Danes and the Swedes sallied forth, in search of Antilles pearls to fasten to their royal crowns. The deeds and misdeeds of European rule gave rise to the differences in the islands, some of them rich, some poor, each one unique.

The majority of today's islanders are descendants of slaves. The European settlers pressed the Amerindian inhabitants into labour, then turned to Africa for the massive workforce required for the cultivation of sugar, the white gold of the 18th century. If the wounds of past tragedy have not quite healed, the blending of peoples has resulted, with time, in a new cultural identity, original and full of optimism. With a colourful language and tropical good humour, the Creole soul pulses rhythmically, finding its utmost expression in zouk music and carnival—and a welcoming glass of *ti-punch*.

Turquoise sea and golden sands, all the
promise of a tropical island.

istockphoto.com / Moore

BRITISH WEST INDIES

Two groups make up the BWI: the Cayman Islands and Turks and Caicos. The sleepy Caymans sprinkle the sea about 300 km (180 miles) northwest of Jamaica. Grand Cayman is the largest of the three, with the majority of the 50,000 population, followed by Cayman Brac and Little Cayman. The Turks and Caicos, locked inside one of the world's most spectacular coral reefs, lie at the end of the Bahamas chain, remote and essentially undiscovered.

Cayman Islands

Most of the points of interest in the islands are on Grand Cayman, an important off-shore financial centre, with some 600 banks and 500 insurance companies in the capital, George Town. The other islands are a loner's paradise. The swimming is great, so is the snorkelling, and the diving has a strong claim to being the best in the Caribbean. For underwater photography, head for Spanish Bay Reef where they have all the gear and expertise.

Beyond the reefs are the big fish such as bluefin, marlin and wahoo. Bonito, amberjack and barracuda are closer to shore and inside the reef you'll land grouper and yellow-tailed snapper. Boats can be rented, ranging from an 18-m (60-ft) yacht to a dinghy.

Grand Cayman

George Town is thriving but very quiet. There are no great sights and although it is pleasant to wander around the well-planned streets (where all the cars stop to let you pass), you will no doubt soon want to head north for **Seven Mile Beach** (a bit shorter, actually), where the big hotels are located and clean white sand stretches to an invitingly blue sea.

To the North

Continue along the coast road to the world's first **Green Turtle Farm**. It provides a legal source of turtle products, such as meat, hide and tortoiseshell, and aims at protecting an endangered species. You can eat turtle on Cayman without suffering pangs of ecological guilt. Afterwards you may as well go to **Hell**. The name refers to the

CAYMAN FLASHBACK

16th century

Columbus discovers the Caymans in 1503, calling the group "Las Tortugas" after the great number of turtles in the surrounding seas. Early Spanish settlers of the Caribbean area rename them the "Caimán" islands, possibly mistaking the native iguanas for alligators.

17th–18th centuries

In 1670 the Caymans are formally ceded to Great Britain by Spain. About the same time, the islands' first permanent settlers arrive, an assortment of debtors, buccaneers hiding from the Royal Navy, deserters from Cromwell's army and sailors shipwrecked on the islands' reefs. They make their living by working small plantations (later with the help of slaves) or by fishing.

19th century–present

By an Act of Parliament in 1863, the Governor and legislature of Jamaica are given certain legislative powers in the Islands. When Jamaica chooses independence in 1962, the Caymans elect to become a British Crown Colony. Today, they are an important international financial centre, with a thriving economy and one of the highest per capita incomes in the Caribbean. Their official status is now that of UK Dependent Territory.

hemis.fr/Renault

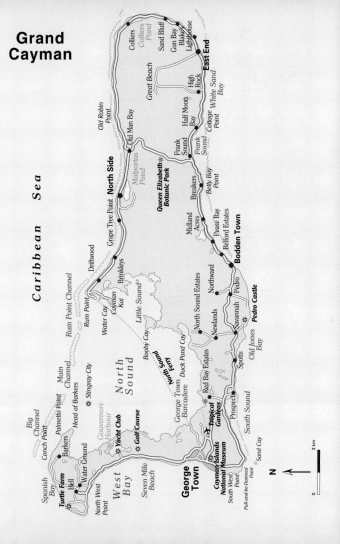

Grand Cayman

Caribbean Sea

Big Channel
Spanish Bay
Conch Point
Palmetto Point
Barkers
Head of Barkers
Water Ground
Main Channel
Gouvernors Harbour
Stingray City
North West Point
West Bay
Hell
Turtle Farm
Seven Mile Beach
Yacht Club
Golf Course

North Sound
Booby Cay
Duck Pond Cay
North Sound Ferry
Barcadere
George Town
Tropical Gardens
Cayman Islands National Museum
Red Bay Estates
Prospect
South Sound
Pull-and-be-Damned Point
South West Point
Sand Cay

Rum Point Channel
Rum Point
Water Cay
Cayman Kai
Little Sound
North Side
Grape Tree Point
Driftwood
Brinkleys

Old Robin Point
Old Man Bay
Malportas Pond
Old Man Bay
Queen Elizabeth Botanic Park
Frank Sound
Frank Sound
Breakers
Betty Bay Point
Midland Acres
Pease Bay
Belford Estates
Bodden Town
North Side Estates
Northward
Newlands
Savannah
Pedro
Pedro Castle
Old Jones Bay
Spotts

Colliers
Colliers Pond
Sand Bluff
Gun Bay
Blakey
Lighthouse
East End
Great Beach
High Rock
Half Moon Bay
Cottage
White Sand Bay
Point

N

0   3 km

Not at all shy, rays come to be fed in the shallow waters of Stingray City.

Philip H. Coblentz

Dantesque area of jagged black limestone formations. The major industry here revolves around selling postcards and stamps and postmarking them to prove you have seen for yourself what life is like in Hell.

Nearby, in the protected waters of North Sound, is **Stingray City**. Stingrays congregate in shallow waters, nuzzling and brushing against the divers feeding them. Visitors can snorkel with the fish or watch from an observatory.

To the East

Pedro Castle was originally built by an Englishman who arrived in the islands in 1765. Local stories also associate it with the pirate Henry Morgan and a 17th-century Spaniard, Pedro Gómez, though there's no proof. Built around 1780 of quarried native stone, the house has been restored by the government as a historic site.

At the **Blow Holes**, sprays of water shoot like geysers through the sea-torn rocks and, further on, the wrecks begin. Over 325 of them have been counted around Grand Cayman. The southernmost, off the east coast, is the *Ridgefield*, perfectly visible from the road. Though the ship was practically empty when it struck a reef in 1943, at least she carried the bonus of 100 cases of beer.

Grand Cayman's central road which strikes off to the left some distance after Betty Bay Point, takes you to the north side and then west as far as **Cayman Kai** and **Rum Point**. The silky sand has been divided up and very pleasant beach houses have been built. The whole landscape shines blue and silver. The gardens are tastefully planted, the holiday houses verging on the luxurious.

Cayman Brac

Uninhabited until 1833, the island now has a population of almost 2000 Cayman Brackers. The name is Gaelic for bluff, a cliff that rises sheer from the water to about 43 m (140 ft). At **Stake Bay**, a museum displays sundry cooking utensils, shipbuilding tools, photographs and other items contributed by the islanders themselves. There are several resorts and condominiums, with services for scuba diving and snorkelling.

Little Cayman

About 200 people live here on 26 sq km (10 sq miles) of silence and fragrant breezes—a haven for escapists. Accommodation here consists of a few small club-style hotels and private cottages. Civilization is slowly encroaching, with a shopping centre and even a bank, but the only excitement is when the plane from Grand Cayman lands on the grass airstrip, bringing guests, mail and gossip.

hemis.fr/Frances

istockphoto.com/Geer

Turks and Caicos

This idyllic string of pearls at the end of the Bahamas chain is sometimes called the last frontier. Ruins of old plantations, mysterious caves and wooden bungalows, shabby but quaint with old age, are as easy to find as the gold and white sand beaches which stretch around the islands.

The Turks Islands were apparently named for a cactus with red blossoms that recalled a Turkish fez, whereas Caicos was probably derived from *cayo*, the Spanish word for small island.

More than 30,000 people live on just eight of the 30 or so islands and cays, over half on Providenciales. Many speak Creole, a legacy of salt trading days with Haiti. Their main revenue now comes from fishing, offshore banking and tourism. The capital of the archipelago, Cockburn Town, is on Grand Turk, a mere 20 sq km (8 sq miles) in area.

Grand Turk

The somewhat rocky eastern coast is countered by undulating dunes on the island's western shore. It enjoys a reputation for

The Providenciales formula for paradise: fabulous seascape and luxury hotels. | Hummingbirds need to eat all day long to survive.

being one of the world's best spots for scuba-diving, and the excellent sport fishing offers everything from sailfish and marlin to wahoos and kingfish. For swimming, the best of its many strands is Governor's Beach on the southwest coast.

Cockburn Town

Known to out-islanders as "the city", the capital provides a striking combination of elegance and hustle and bustle: its venerable 200-year-old limestone church of St Thomas sits happily in the lap of the islands' business centre.

The best way to see the town is by donkey carriage. The handsome buggy, elaborately carved, will take you in style through the historic areas of Duke Street, the main thoroughfare, and Front Street, where three-storey houses of wood and limestone in typical West Indian style line the seafront. Stop off at the old **Victoria Public Library** to see its fascinating collection of reference books relating to local history.

On Front Street, the **National Museum** occupies Guinep Lodge, an 18th-century residence. Its key exhibit, covering most of the ground floor, is the Molasses Reef Wreck, an early 16th-century Spanish caravel. The museum also documents the salt industry and displays artefacts of the Lucayan Indians.

The Cays

Pennington Cay, Gibbs Cay and Round Cay have sanctuaries where you'll see some interesting bird and butterfly species. **Salt Cay**, 14 km (9 miles) from Grand Turk, is the most charming and atmospheric of all the salt islands. Easily accessible by boat and only five minutes away by air, it has fine beaches and old windmills next to the long-abandoned salt ponds. On the west side there are two small villages. At the southern tip of the island the sea tends to be rough.

Caicos Islands

Humpback whales put on a spectacular show from January to March when they wend their way, during their southern migration, through the Turks Island Passage, 36 km (21 miles) wide, separating the Turks and the more westerly Caicos.

By boat or a 10-minute flight, you can hop over this passage from Grand Turk to **South Caicos**, the most populated island in the days of the salt trade. Today it counts a little more than 1000 inhabitants. Lively Cockburn Harbour, the only town, is the main fishing port for the islands.

Middle Caicos (or Grand Caicos) is the largest of the islands, but only sparsely populated. On the north coast there are extraordinary limestone caves, worth a

TURKS AND CAICOS FLASHBACK

16th century
In 1512 Spanish explorer Ponce de León discovers Grand Turk, inhabited by Lucayan Indians.

17th century
The islands are used as pirates' hideaways. Using slave labour, Bermudian traders, the first whites to settle permanently here, begin collecting natural sea salt for sale to the British colonies in America.

18th century
Despite a 1710 Spanish invasion and three French invasions, the Bermudians keep returning to the islands and rebuilding their salt pans. In 1766, the Turks and Caicos are placed under the control of the Bahamas, a British colony. During the American Revolution, British loyalists flee to the Caicos, where they plant sisal and cotton.

19th century
The islands separate from the Bahamas in 1848, but in 1874 become a dependency of Jamaica.

20th century–present
John Glenn, the first American to orbit the planet, splashes down off the coast of Grand Turk in 1962. That year the islands win independence from Jamaica but are linked for administrative purposes with the Bahamas. In 1972 they receive their own governor as a British Crown Colony. Hotels spring up, including luxury resorts. In August 2009, the UK suspends self-government after allegations of ministerial corruption. The incumbent governor is vested with the prerogative of ministerial government and the House of Assembly for two years.

flickr.com/Ali West

visit to see the reflections of sta-lactites and stalagmites in the clear, still salt ponds. In 1977, American archaeologists came to the islands to explore the caves and ruins near Bambarra and Lorimers and discovered artefacts and relics of the Lucayan and Arawak Indians, the islands' earliest settlers.

North Caicos, the "Garden Island" is known for its growing tourist development along a 9-km (6-mile) beach and opposite the best bonefishing waters. The inhabitants are shared between four villages: Bottle Creek on the eastern edge, Whitby in the north, Kew in the centre and Sandy Point in the northwest.

Privately owned, **Pine Cay** has one of the world's most exquisite beaches, stretching for 4 km (2.5 miles) opposite the Caicos Cays National Underwater Park. Hiking along trails on the island, you'll encounter Amerindian and British colonial ruins. Nearby Water Cay and Little Water Cay are rich with shells for collectors.

Most of the major tourist infrastructure is concentrated on the island of **Providenciales**, simply referred to by the locals as "Provo". It has been able to achieve a certain degree of self-sufficiency thanks to development, small farming operations and its own spiny lobster and conch-processing plants.

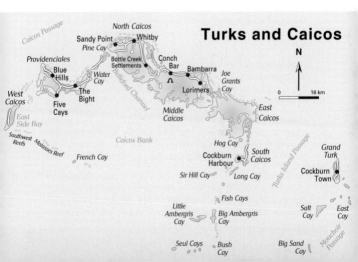

THE HARD FACTS

Airports. Owen Roberts International Airport (GCM) is 2 km (1 mile) east of George Town, and Gerard Smith Airport (CYB) on Cayman Brac is 8 km (5 miles) from West End. Grand Turk (GDT) is 3 km (2 miles) south of Cockburn Town. There are international airstrips on South Caicos (XSC) and Providenciales (PLS).

Banks. *Grand Cayman*: Monday to Thursday 9 a.m.–4 p.m.; Friday 9 a.m.–4.30 p.m. Little Cayman's bank opens Monday and Thursday only. *Turks and Caicos*: Monday to Thursday 8.30 a.m.–3.30 p.m.; Fridays 8.30 a.m.–4.30 p.m.

Climate. The Caymans bask in a warm, tropical climate throughout the year. High temperatures are moderated by trade winds. The rainy season runs from May to October, but showers are generally brief. On Turks and Caicos, the climate is very dry, although it's somewhat more humid in North Caicos. Average temperature 75–85°F (24–29°C) from November to May and higher between June and October. The constant trade-winds keep things comfortable. The hurricane season runs from June to October.

Clothing. Pack lightweight cottons and linens and a raincoat or umbrella for the the rainy season. Warmer clothes may be needed on cooler evenings.

Communications. The islands are linked to the US network. Country code for Cayman Islands 1 345, for Turks and Caicos 1 649. The international access code from the Cayman Islands is 00; from Turks and Caicos 001. Internet connection is available at most large hotels and Internet cafés.

Customs Allowance. Free import of 200 cigarettes or 25 cigars or 250 g tobacco, 1 litre spirits, 4 litres wine or 9 litres beer for visitors over 18 (Cayman Islands); 200 cigarettes or 50 cigars or 125 g tobacco, 1 litre spirits or 2 litres wine (Turks and Caicos).

Driving. Traffic drives on the left. A good road network connects the coastal towns of all three main Cayman islands, where drivers must be over 25 and speed limits are strictly enforced. To hire a car, a temporary local driving licence is required, issued on presentation of a valid national licence. Four-wheel drive vehicles are available, and you can also rent a moped, motorbike or bicycle. On Turks and Caicos, about one-fifth of the roads are surfaced. A limited selection of car hire is available on Grand Turk, Providenciales and North and South Caicos.

Electricity. 110 volts AC, 50 Hz. Plugs have two flat pins.

Holidays. *All islands*: January 1, Good Friday, Easter Monday, December 25–26. *Cayman Islands*: February–March, Ash Wednesday (40 days before Easter); May, Discovery Day; June, Queen's Official Birthday; July, Constitution Day; November, Remembrance Day. *Turks and Caicos*: March 10, Commonwealth Day; May, National Heroes' Day; June, HM The Queen's Birthday; August, Emancipation Day; September, National Youth Day; October, Columbus Day; International Human Rights Day.

Language. English is the official language, with minority local dialects also spoken, and some Creole on Turks and Caicos.

Money. The Cayman Islands dollar (CI$ or KYD) is divided into 100 cents. Coins range from 1 to 25 cents, banknotes from 1 to 100 dollars. Prices are usually quoted in Cayman dollars, but shops will also accept US and Canadian dollars. On Turks and Caicos the US dollar is used. Major credit cards and travellers cheques in US dollars are widely accepted by most hotels, better restaurants and shops.

Time. GMT −5. Turks and Caicos observe daylight saving time: GMT −4 from first Sunday in April to last Saturday in October.

Tipping. 10–15% is normal for most services. Hotels and apartments state the specific amount or add it automatically. Restaurant bills usually add 10–15% in lieu of tipping.

Transport. On Grand Cayman, a regular bus service runs between George Town and the West Bay residential area, connecting most of the hotels along Seven Mile Beach, and also to Bodden Town, North Side and East End. There are plenty of taxis. On Turks and Caicos, taxis are available at the airports, but the supply may be limited and sharing is often necessary.

Water. Bottled mineral water is available. On Turks and Caicos, all running water should be regarded as potentially contaminated: water used for brushing your teeth or making ice should be boiled or sterilized.

The Jamaicans adore bright colours, as you'll see from their clothes and their homes.

hemis.fr / Du Boisberranger

JAMAICA

Jamaica lies some 150 km (90 miles) south of Cuba and is the third-largest Caribbean island after Cuba and Hispaniola (shared between Haiti and the Dominican Republic): 235 km (145 miles) long and 82 km (51 miles) at its widest part. The capital and most important commercial centre is Kingston, situated on the south coast. An array of stunning resorts with majestic sand beaches extends along the north coast. The original inhabitants, peaceful Arawak Indians, called it Xamayaca, Land of Wood and Water.

Kingston Area

If the island is mostly an exotic Eden of sighing breezes, swaying palms and turquoise seas, not so its capital, which is neither pretty nor charming, but everything you would expect a busy Caribbean port city to be—crowded, lively, and occasionally even aggressive.

Kingston throbs to the sound of reggae and calypso. Dread-locked Rastafarians amble by, while the women swirl past in long, colourful skirts, with their heads covered. Exotic smells fill the air, which hums with the song of the island's 200 species of birds. And ever present in the distance is the outline of the Blue Mountains, wreathed with trailing mists.

Founded by survivors of the Port Royal earthquake of 1692, Kingston soon expanded and became the seat of trade and principal Jamaican port. Despite frequent damage from earthquakes and fire over its 300 years of development, Kingston still has some fine colonial-style buildings—relics of a bygone era. The city falls into two sections—Downtown Kingston and New Kingston, where the ground rises towards the cooler, airy foothills of the Blue Mountains.

New Kingston

This is a modern development of hotels, banks, offices and shops in the uptown area. Some of the city's loveliest houses are near at hand, with lace-like verandas and

JAMAICA FLASHBACK

15th–16th centuries
Columbus sights the north coast of Jamaica in 1494 and lands in Montego Bay. During his fourth voyage (1502–04) he is marooned for a year at St Ann's Bay. In 1510 the Spanish found a settlement nearby, Sevilla la Nueva. Fever drives the settlers to the south coast, the site of today's Spanish Town. During the 150 years of Spanish colonial rule, the originally 60,000-strong Arawaks are wiped out by disease and massacre. African slaves are brought in to replace them as a labour force.

17th century
The British land in Kingston Harbour (1655) and capture Jamaica. The Spanish governor heads for the hills, where he carries on a guerrilla resistance for five years. The Treaty of Madrid (1670) sets an official seal on England's claim to Jamaica. Escaping slaves who take refuge in the hills—the Maroons—harass the British.

18th century
A prosperous era of sugar and slavery. Uprisings are common; the planters fear for their lives and fortify their homes. In 1739 the British sign a treaty with the Maroons, granting them certain privileges and independence, and thus putting a stop to the intermittent warfare. By 1785, Jamaica has a population of 25,000 whites and 250,000 slaves.

19th century
Jamaica's last and most serious slave rebellion occurs in Montego Bay in 1831. Slavery is abolished by Parliament in 1833 but the system does not actually die out for another 50 years. As the sugar industry begins its decline, the living conditions of the emancipated slaves grow ever worse, and a minor revolt in 1865 to obtain justice meets with swift reprisals. Jamaica is named a Crown Colony in 1866.

20th century–present
Thanks to the newly developed banana trade, the discovery of bauxite and growing tourism, the economy experiences a lift. Jamaica is granted its own constitution and self-government in 1944. On August 6, 1962, the island becomes independent but remains part of the British Commonwealth and a lively democracy.

wooden decoration. On Hope Road, **Devon House** is one of the finest. It was built in 1881 by George Stiebel, one of the first black millionaires in the Caribbean. The government has refurbished it in the style of different periods in Jamaican history, and it is often used as a backdrop for wedding photos. The staff quarters have been turned into craft shops, and the restaurant is famous for its Jamaican cuisine.

The **Bob Marley Museum**, 56 Hope Road, has been set up in the reggae musician's former home and studio, and documents his life and works. He died in Miami in 1981. The Tuff Gong record label was founded here by The Wailers in 1970.

An eastward jaunt along Hope and Old Hope roads takes you to the **Hope Botanical Gardens**, the largest in the Caribbean.

Downtown

The waterfront's broad boulevards, skyscrapers and the showpiece **Conference Centre** are sparkling new. In the Kingston Mall, Jamaica's **National Gallery** comprises contemporary paintings, Spanish and English colonial art, and Taino artefacts.

Iron forged into delicate lacework on a colonial house in Port Antonio. | Bob Marley's recording studio in Kingston.

hemis.fr/Frumm

Huber/Pavan

Craft Market

At the west end of Harbour Street is Kingston's Craft Market, taking up a big modern building. This is the spot to look for basketry, carving, embroidery and thousands of examples of straw weaving.

Parish Church

Kingston Parish Church on South Parade warrants a visit. The original brick building of 1699 was destroyed in the 1907 earthquake, but the present structure still contains the black marble gravestone of Admiral Benbow, who died in 1702 after a battle with the French.

Blue Mountains

The best way to go is via Papine, Guava Ridge and Mavis Bank. Start early; don't forget to take a

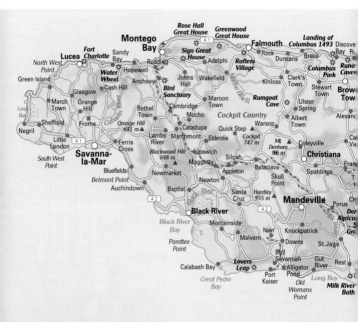

sweater (the air is cool) and strong shoes. There are some delightful walks in the area and a feeling of splendid isolation as pale mountain mists wreathe and swirl over plunging valleys and lush vegetation.

Mavis Bank is the departure point for the climb, a tough, three-hour trek up to Blue Mountain Peak, 7,402 ft (2,256 m). The classic hike involves starting out

at 2 a.m. so that you arrive at the summit in time for a sensational sunrise. The more northerly road to Newcastle and Hardwar Gap brings you within range of Holly-well National Forest, an ideal spot for bird-watching.

Port Royal
To get to Port Royal, either take a water taxi from Pier No. 2 or drive there on the Palisadoes

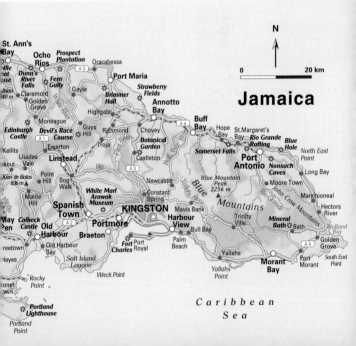

hemis.fr/Frances

Huber

Many trails in the Blue Mountains follow the paths made by the Maroons. | View over Fort Charles.

road. The land route passes Long Mountain which sports a Martello tower on its slopes and a fort at its foot.

In the late 17th century, Boston and Port Royal were the largest cities of the English colonies in the New World. Port Royal, built on a sandy peninsula, was known as "the wickedest city on earth". Here the pirates caroused, rum and money flowed freely, pleasure was sweet, and death often quick and violent. And then, suddenly, on June 7, 1692, two-thirds of the town sank beneath the sea. Violent earthquakes and a tidal wave toppled the buildings and claimed the lives of over a thousand people. Some claim that on stormy days you can still hear the doleful tolling of submerged church bells.

Excavations of the underwater city began in the 1980s, mainly focusing on buildings on Lime Street, inland from the harbour. It is one of the richest 17th-century archaeological sites in the world.

St Peter's Church

Built in 1725, it replaced the earlier churches which disappeared in the earthquake and ensuing fire. Outside is the tomb of Louis Galdy, a French refugee from religious persecution. During the famous earthquake he was swallowed into a yawning crack in the ground and thrown out again into the sea, where he swam to a boat and managed to save himself.

Fort Charles

Once commanded by Nelson, this is the only one of the six original forts to have survived Port Royal's manifold disasters. It was founded in 1656 and named after Charles II of England. The prow-shaped fort once stood at the water's edge, but land movements have shifted it to an inland position. It houses an interesting maritime museum.

Archaeological Museum

The Naval Hospital, built in 1819 mainly for sufferers from yellow fever, has found a new lease of life as a museum displaying objects recovered from the sunken city—candelabra, bottles, pewter plates, chamber pots, silver, bone and ivory articles—along with artefacts from the excavations of Arawak sites.

Spanish Town

The Spanish called it Villa de La Vega, "town on the plain". The old centre is full of charm and history. Just outside town, the **White Marl Arawak Museum** houses some of the most important Arawak finds in the country.

Spanish Town itself is set on the banks of the River Cobre. The only thing Spanish about it now is the name, but the **Cathedral Church of St James** stands on the site of a Spanish chapel demolished by Oliver Cromwell's soldiers.

The British designed a graceful little square for the town centre. There stood the governor's residence, **King's House**, burnt out but rebuilt now to house an archaeological museum. The stables are home to the **People's Craft and Technology Museum**.

On the north side of the square is a John Bacon memorial to Admiral George Rodney, who saved Jamaica from French invasion in 1782. On the south side stands the 19th-century court-house. The colonnaded red brick and wood structure, east, is the House of Assembly, erected in the 1760s.

Who are they? Today's almost 2.7 million Jamaicans are a rich cultural and racial mix, bringing together strands of African and European culture, along with Arab, Chinese and Indian influences; they underline the truth of the motto "out of many races one people". The same phenomenon applies to the language of the island. Jamaicans of every skin hue speak English, but they communicate more often in a dialect that is a rich mix of English, Spanish and African— to outsiders it's incomprehensible.

hemis.fr/Frumm

Effortless rafting on the Rio Grande is not to be missed.

hemis.fr/Cintract

Resorts

Each of these resorts, dotted along the north coast of the island, has in its way contributed to Jamaica's reputation as a prime holiday destination. The earliest testimonial to Jamaica was given in 1494, when Christopher Columbus landed on the island: he described it as "the fairest island that eyes have beheld".

Port Antonio

Regularly refreshed by rain showers, Port Antonio, on the northeast coast, about 100 km (60 miles) from Kingston, is one of the greenest spots in Jamaica. It was an early mecca for tourism, well before anyone had even heard of Montego Bay or Ocho Rios. They have since surpassed Port Antonio in tourist numbers, but this town, in contrast, offers a feeling of exclusivity and charm.

Cradled by the arms of the Blue Mountains, Port Antonio has two superb harbours, divided by the Titchfield Peninsula. On its tip rises Fort George (which may be visited), built to protect the original settlement; today its walls enclose a school. No one has yet thought up more imaginative names for East Harbour and West Harbour, flanked by Navy Island, once owned by the film star Errol Flynn. The waters off Port Antonio are noted for deep-sea fishing.

Bonnie View

A walk up to Bonnie View is rewarded with a splendid panorama of the town and harbours. Head for the lighthouse and you will see Folly Estate, an enormous dilapidated mansion of 1905. Locals relate that the house collapsed when the owner, the American billionaire Alfred Mitchell, arrived with his new bride. The truth is that in 1938 the roof caved in, after the house had fallen prey to sea salt, which corroded the iron reinforcing rods.

Rafting on the Rio Grande. No visit to Jamaica is complete without a raft trip down the Rio Grande, between the slopes of the Blue Mountains. Originally, the bamboo rafts were used by banana plantation owners to transport their produce to the port. On holidays the planters liked to coast along with family and friends. It was Errol Flynn who first hit on the idea of having a raft fitted with seats to make the ride more comfortable. A qualified rafter navigates the rapids, giving you the chance to marvel at the luxuriant jungle scenery. A three-hour trip departs from Grant's Level and glides beneath the foliage to Rafter's Rest, equipped with a bar and restaurant, marking the end of the 7-mile (11-km) trip.

Nonsuch Caves

A fairly easy expedition 8 km (5 miles) inland from Port Antonio, the caves are situated at the Seven Hills of Athenry, a working fruit plantation. From here there is a fine view to the coast and up to Blue Mountain Peak. Since the rock in the caves was formed under the sea, you'll spot some marine fossils.

Blue Lagoon

Breathtaking views can be enjoyed at many points along the coastline, which offers a number of tempting white beaches. Don't miss a visit to Blue Lagoon, also known as Blue Hole, southeast of Port Antonio. Translucent water of the deepest ultramarine lies surrounded by dark vegetation.

Ocho Rios Region

The region embraces a golden strip about 100 km (60 miles) long between Annotto and Discovery Bay and is considered one of the most important tourist havens in Jamaica.

Port Maria and Oracabessa

The road west from Annotto Bay leads to Port Maria, an old banana port, where there are some lovely views over the shoreline. Inland lies Brimmer Hall, a famous plantation house. You can explore the grounds on a "jitney", a tractor-pulled open buggy.

Both Port Maria and Oracabessa, another banana port, gained fame through two celebrated British writers who settled in the region. Ian Fleming married in Port Maria's town hall and wrote his James Bond novels at his estate, *Goldeneye* in Oracabessa. His *Dr No* was filmed in Jamaica, part of it in the old bauxite factory at Ocho Rios.

Sir Noël Coward's home, **Firefly**, stands on a stunning headland near Port Maria overlooking the sea. He died here and is buried at the bottom of the garden under a marble slab. The house has been restored and is now a museum displaying theatrical memorabilia and some of Coward's paintings. Just below the house is an Arawak site that has been partly excavated and can be visited.

Prospect Plantation

A road turns inland towards this working farm that, like Brimmer Hall, is visited by jitney—or on horseback. An experienced guide leads you along marked trails through plantations and cattle raising land.

Harmony Hall

Some of the best of Jamaican arts and crafts are displayed in this former great house of a small pimento plantation.

Ocho Rios Town

In Ocho Rios proper, you have a vast choice of activities: scuba diving, deep-sea fishing, golf, horseriding, shopping sprees in Pineapple Place, Coconut Grove or Ocean Village, or just some relaxing swimming and sunbathing. At the **Coyaba River Garden**, riverside paths wander past waterfalls and pools filled with koi carp and turtles. Its museum has a collection of pre-Columbian artefacts, while the gallery displays contemporary art of Jamaica. The **Shaw Park Gardens**, besides acres of lawns and terraces of tropical flora, birds and waterfalls, offer a splendid view of Ocho Rios Bay and the surrounding countryside.

Dunn's River Falls

Along the coast to the west, this is the loveliest, most refreshing spot around. Clear, cool water from the rainforest comes cascading down over limestone terraces through pools to the sea. You can climb the falls assisted by experienced guides, or take the steps with handrails and wooden observation decks. Once a week, music and dancing begin in early evening, along with a Jamaican "feast".

St Ann's Bay

This is the capital of the parish of the same name. You can watch polo at Drax Hall east of town;

hemis.fr

You can climb from the beach all the way to the top of Dunn's River Falls.

matches are held every Saturday. At the gem factory, you will be shown all the steps that it takes to transform a raw stone into a finished piece of jewellery.

To the west is the site of Jamaica's first Spanish settlement, Sevilla Nueva, founded in 1509. Columbus had landed nearby a few years earlier, an event that his native city of Genoa commemorated in 1957 with a gift of a bronze monument. Archaeological excavations have revealed only a few fragments of ancient stones.

Françoise Ohayon

Fans of reggae music head inland, via Claremont, Bonneville and Alderton, to Nine Miles, site of the **Bob Marley Mausoleum**, where the king of reggae is buried with his guitar. Adorned with stained-glass windows, it contrasts bizarrely with the adjacent humble hut where this international cult figure spent his childhood.

istockphoto.com/Valjamaa

The parish church of St James in Montego Bay.

Runaway Bay

A line-up of hotels fringes the shores of Runaway Bay. The limestone **Runaway Caves**, first used by the Arawak Indians, later became a pirate and smugglers' haunt and then a place of refuge for runaway slaves.

A visit to the caves also includes an eerie boat ride in the **Green Grotto**, 36 m (120 ft) underground, with stalagmites, stalactites and a tiny lake. It is fed by channels connected to the sea, and the water level rises and falls with the tides. A nightclub has been built inside the cave, and you can fish in another lake, outside.

This part of the coast is replete with memories of Columbus. The great navigator is said to have first sailed into **Discovery Bay**, though he did not necessarily land here. As he found no fresh water, he named the place Puerto Seco, "dry harbour", then carried on westwards to the next horseshoe-shaped bay, at the mouth of the river he called Rio Bueno. At the west side of Discovery Bay, on the cliff road to Montego Bay, lies **Columbus Park**. Here the points of interest are the many relics of Jamaica's early history, such as an old waterwheel and some large sugar cauldrons.

Along the whole coast are beautiful white sand beaches, notably Braco and Trelawny.

Montego Bay

MoBay, as it is familiarly called, entered the touristic scene early in the 20th century when a certain Dr McCatty, ahead of his time, advocated the bracing virtues of salt-water bathing. Nowadays nobody doubts the benefits, and Montego Bay has become part of Caribbean history. The region has much to offer: superb hotels, well-stocked shopping plazas, excellent golf courses, plenty of other sports and dreamy beaches.

Montego Bay falls naturally into three areas: the town itself, the coastal strip with hotels and shopping plazas, and the hills behind.

Montego Bay Town

The Cage, right in the centre of town on Sam Sharpe Square, dates from 1807. It used to be a gaol for runaway slaves. On Sundays, the plantation slaves were allowed to come to town to sell their produce but they were supposed to leave after a bell rang at 2 o'clock. Any slaves still on the streets after the second bell at 3 were locked up in the Cage.

Also on Sam Sharpe Square stand the remains of the **Old Court House**, which bears the date 1804 over its main doorway. This was the scene—after the slave rebellion of 1831—of hundreds of trials and sentences carried out in a summary fashion. Those found guilty—like one of their leaders Sam Sharpe himself—were strung up outside the courthouse to serve as examples.

The handsome Georgian parish **church of St James** was built at the end of the 18th century and was faithfully reconstructed after an earthquake in 1957. Inside you'll find fine mahogany furnishings and two monuments by the prominent British sculptor John Bacon (1740–99); outside are tropical gardens.

Down at the end of Market Street is the open-air **St James' Craft Market**, where basketware, straw goods, embroidery and wood-carving are featured. Duty-free shops abound all over Montego Bay, but the biggest grouping of them is found in Freeport, on a small peninsula west of the city.

Martha Brae

The Montego Bay area stretches 42 km (26 miles) east to the Martha Brae, a rafting river like the Rio Grande. The trip along the winding waterway begins in **Rafter's Village**, where you find picnic facilities, souvenir shops, and refreshments. Feathery bamboo fringes the river as you drift through banana plantations, fields of sugar cane and yams. Birds a-plenty—small green parakeets, woodpeckers and the energetic bananaquit—serenade you on your way. The journey ends at **Rock**, and a bus brings visitors back to the starting point.

Estates

Greenwood House, built in the 18th century, boasts fine furniture, early musical instruments, as well as one or two well-authenticated ghosts.

Rose Hall, restored from a ruin at great expense, is said to be the home of the infamous "white witch", a restless young woman who killed all three of her husbands, as well as miscellaneous lovers. With its mahogany panelling, furniture in exotic woods and superb staircase, the 1760-built mansion figures still as one of the most beautiful in Jamaica.

Inland from Montego Bay, near **Anchovy**, you can observe and photograph rare birds such as the orange quit and the doctor bird at **Lisa Salmon's Bird Sanctuary**. Mango hummingbirds fly down to drink from hand-held bottles. Feeding takes place around 4 p.m.

Cockpit Country

Inland is a landscape like something out of another world: huge potholes and sharp peaks carved out of the limestone, all covered with dense vegetation. This was one of the places where runaway slaves could hide out from the British, and their descendants still live in Maroon villages such as **Accompong**. The region is best visited on an organized trip from Montego Bay. You can also take a bus trip to the **Appleton Estate**, a plantation and rum distillery.

Negril

In the 1960s, Negril, on the west coast, was a simple village the hippies headed for, to enjoy an offbeat, uncomplicated life "away from it all". Now it's a fully fledged resort area.

On the way there from Montego Bay, you pass through the

hemis.fr / Rieger

Carrying heavy baskets in this way does wonders for one's poise.

pretty port of **Lucea**, which once handled sugar. It is overlooked by Fort Charlotte, open for visits.

Negril's harbour goes by the name of Bloody Bay, dating back to whaling days. It's an appealing beach, but can't hold a candle to the long stretch of warm, shimmering sand at **Long Bay** further south.

Negril's west end, between South Negril River and the lighthouse, is especially attractive. The indentations in the rocky coastline make for good swimming and snorkelling.

THE HARD FACTS

Airport. Norman Manley International (KIN) lies 17 km (11 miles) south-east of Kingston. Sangster International Airport at Montego Bay (MBJ) is 3 km (2 miles north of the city. Domestic flights operate between Tinson Pen (KTP) in Kingston, Negril (NEG), Boscobel (OCJ) in Ocho Rios and Ken Jones (POT) in Port Antonio.

Banks. Open Monday to Thursday 9 a.m. –2 p.m.; Friday 9 a.m.–noon and 2–5 p.m. Keep all currency exchange receipts to reconvert your Jamaican dollars when you leave the island.

Climate. Tropical all year. Temperate in mountain areas. The rainy months are May and October, but there can be rainfall at any time during the year. Evenings tend to be cool. The hurricane season is from June to October.

Clothing. Casual clothing is the rule. During the day shorts and beachwear are fine for the resorts and beaches, but to stroll in town you will need something dressier. A broad-brimmed hat is useful against the powerful sun. Bring along a jacket or pullover for cool breezes, and for the mountains, warm clothing and sturdy shoes are indispensable.

Communications. Jamaica is linked to the US network. Country code: 1 876. The international access code is 011. You will find Internet services in most large hotels, and there are Internet cafés in the towns.

Customs Allowance. The following goods may be imported by visitors aged minimum 18 without incurring customs duty: 200 cigarettes or 50 cigars or 225 g of tobacco; 1 litre of spirits (excluding rum); 1 litre wine; 150 g of perfume.

Driving. Traffic drives on the left. Big towns, and the airports, have car rental facilities; a consumption tax of 15per cent is imposed. A UK, US or Canadian driving licence is valid.

Electricity. 110 volts AC, 50 Hz with sockets for single-phase 2-pin plugs. Many hotels are also equipped with 220 volts AC, 50 Hz and sockets for single-phase 3-pin plugs.

Holidays. January 1, New Year's Day; February–March Ash Wednesday (40 days before Easter); Good Friday; Easter Monday; May 23, Labour Day; August, Emancipation Day; August 6, Independence Day; October, National Heroes' Day; December 25–26, Christmas.

Money. The Jamaican dollar (J$ or JMD) is divided into 100 cents. Coins range from 1 cent to J$20, banknotes from J$50 to 1000. American currency is also widely accepted. Credit Cards and travellers cheques are accepted almost everywhere. Travellers cheques in US dollars are recommended.

Shops. Open generally Monday to Saturday 9–5 p.m. Half-day closing Wednesday in Kingston, Thursday elsewhere.

Time. GMT–5, all year round.

Tipping. Most Jamaican hotels and restaurants add a service charge of 10%; if not, you are expected to leave 10–15%. Chambermaids, waiters, hotel bellboys, porters and taxi drivers all expect tips.

Transport. There is reliable bus service in Montego Bay; timetables for trans-island travel are more haphazard. Coach and minibus tours can be booked at most hotels. Not all taxis are metered, so it is best to check standard charges prior to the trip and agree on a fare before setting off. A number of local operators run yacht tours, as well as cruises.

Water. The tap water in hotels and cities is filtered and chlorinated and is safe to drink. Off the beaten track, it is possible to come across untreated water, which will be clearly marked as unfit for consumption. Bottled mineral water is widely available, and you may want to bring along water-purifying tablets for drinking tap water. Never drink from streams or rivers.

A fort with a view—the imposing Castillo El Morro.

PUERTO RICO

Most visitors to Puerto Rico get no further than San Juan—especially the glitzy strip of hotel-lined beach that stretches from Isla Verde, past Condado (the "action" centre) to Old San Juan. You can count on the sun and fun, but while you're here, savour, too, the island's Spanish heritage. Take time to wander around Old San Juan, the city's beautifully restored colonial section. Inspect the formidable old forts; visit the late-Gothic churches; see the Spanish-style plazas, balconied houses, wrought-iron grilles and arcaded patios.

San Juan

Old Town

You can take in the high spots of Old San Juan in an intensive half-day tour. But don't try to see it all—there's too much to cover in a single round. A good place to start is the harbour, where you can call in at La Casita to pick up brochures and maps at the tourist information office.

Paseo de la Princesa

The 19th-century esplanade, recently restored at great expense, leads west then north from the port, following the city wall. The former prison, **La Princesa**, has been transformed into a gallery of modern art.

Overlooking San Juan Bay, **La Fortaleza**—"the Fortress"—is a grand mansion built in 1540 for defence against the Carib Indians. But as more advanced enemies appeared, the old fort became a military white elephant, impressive to see but vulnerable. This was lucky for the governors of Puerto Rico, who have lived and worked in the 40-room mansion for over 400 years.

The esplanade ends at **San Juan Gate**, the oldest portal in the solid city wall. Visiting dignitaries used to land at this spot to be escorted in procession up to the cathedral.

Around the Cathedral

The pink cathedral of San Juan was thoroughly rebuilt in the 19th

PUERTO RICO FLASHBACK

15th–16th centuries

The peaceful Taíno Indians welcome Christopher Columbus, accompanied by nobleman Juan Ponce de León, to their island of Borinquén on November 19, 1493. Columbus calls it San Juan. In 1508, Ponce de León founds a Spanish settlement, but its site proves to be unhealthy and indefensible. The colonists move to another bay, Puerto Rico ("Rich Port"). The two names are somehow exchanged. The Spaniards soon exhaust the island's gold and put the Indians to work growing sugar cane. Slaves are imported from West Africa and fortifications are built. Sir Francis Drake attacks the town in 1595 — and is forced to retreat. The English fare better a few years later when the Earl of Cumberland shrewdly outflanks and lays siege to the fortress of El Morro. The British take the fort but lose the island: they are routed by an epidemic of yellow fever and dysentery.

17th–18th centuries

The Dutch sail into the harbour and march into the deserted city. But El Morro refuses to surrender and the disgruntled Dutch depart after setting fire to San Juan. The Spaniards refortify, building a defensive wall around the town. The British make one more attempt in 1797, surrounding and blockading the city. Then suddenly the British withdraw — frightened, the legend goes, by a torchlight parade of praying women, which they mistake for Spanish reinforcements.

19th century

The repressive military rule of Spain is disturbed by a small insurrection in Puerto Rico in 1868. The insurgents are quickly suppressed but the weary Spanish decide to change their tactics and ease the tension. In 1872, slavery is abolished; in 1897, the island is granted autonomy. Eight months later, the United States, involved in the Spanish-American War, lands troops on the south coast and takes Puerto Rico.

20th century–present

Puerto Ricans are made US citizens in 1917 and given more say in internal affairs. Since 1952, Puerto Rico has been a self-governing Commonwealth, freely associated with the United States. The chance to become a US state was rejected in a referendum. One-third of all Puerto Ricans live in the US, which still leaves 4 million on the island.

century, having been twice damaged by hurricanes. Only the circular staircase and some adjoining rooms with Gothic ceilings remain from the 1540 structure. The marble tomb near the transept holds the remains of Ponce de León.

El Convento Hotel (off to the right as you leave the cathedral) was once a Carmelite convent. Today it welcomes guests to its handsome restored rooms and restaurant, originally the convent's chapel.

Plaza de Armas

Hundreds of years ago, citizen-soldiers used to drill in Plaza de Armas, the central square of Old San Juan. Later the plaza became a favourite meeting place with band concerts. Restored in 1988, it now has a grandstand, pavilion, water fountain and snack bar.

The highlight of the **Casa Alcaldía** (City Hall) is its vast assembly room upstairs with a chequerboard marble floor, dignified chandeliers and a grand piano. It opens onto an arcaded balcony, tailormade for an election night victory speech. The building was remodelled in the 1840s.

Plaza de San José

The statue of Juan Ponce de León in his armour was cast from British cannon, captured after an unsuccessful attack on San Juan

in 1797. Ponce de León was buried in the church of San José until 1908, when he was moved to the cathedral. This all-white building was begun in 1532. It's a fine sight, and, unusual for the tropics, a rare example of late-Gothic style brought to the New World. The great vaulted ceilings date from the 16th century.

Also on the plaza is the **Pablo Casals Museum**. Here you discover the much-treasured memorabilia of the great Spanish cellist, who spent his last years in Puerto Rico. Exhibits include his cello and videotapes of Puerto Rico's annual Festival Casals.

The **Dominican Convent** once gave refuge to women and children hiding out from the Carib Indians. More recently, it was the headquarters of the US Army's Antilles Command. Now the public can enjoy the tranquillity of its expansive, double-decker patio, a splendid example of Spanish colonial design.

Puerto Rico's woodcarvers are renowned for their *santos*, simple religious figurines. Some admirable historic *santos* may be seen in **La Casa de los Contrafuertes** (House of the Buttresses), a fortress-like mansion thought to be the oldest private residence in San Juan. Two other exhibits share the premises: an old, reconstructed apothecary shop and a graphic arts show.

Plaza del Quinto Centenario

The "Quincentennial Plaza", a park and cultural complex, was inaugurated in 1992 on the 500th anniversary of Columbus's arrival in the New World. Its focal point is an exuberant fountain.

Nearby is the **Cuartel de Ballajá**, once the residential quarter for Spanish troops and their families. Here, the former asylum for the poor now houses the **Institute of Puerto Rican Culture** with its changing exhibits, while the old bar-

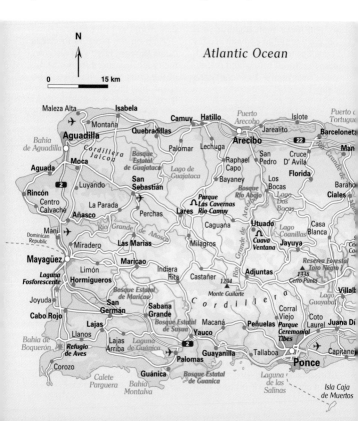

racks contain the **Museum of the Americas** and their eye-catching collections of folk art.

Casa Blanca

The US Army again shows proof of good taste in choosing sites for its headquarters in the Casa Blanca (White House), a sprawling, Spanish-style structure with delicious little gardens. The local commander was billeted here until 1966. Now housing the **Juan Ponce de León Museum**, filled with

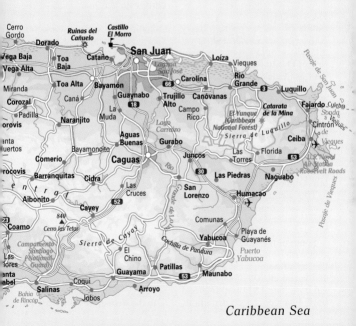

Puerto Rico

Caribbean Sea

furniture and relics of the colonial days, the house looks as it might have done back in 1523 when Ponce de León's son-in-law moved in. Also within these walls is the **Taino Indian Ethno-Historic Museum**, documenting the life and culture of the island's first inhabitants.

Heading back downhill from Calle San Sebastián, the most pleasant route is the set of step streets—just for pedestrians. Tropical plants add to the charm.

Plaza de Colon

South of the cathedral, lively Calle Fortaleza leads east to yet another installation of the Institute of Puerto Rican Culture—**La Casa del Callejón** (House of the Alley), an 18th-century mansion with two museums. On the ground floor you'll find colonial architecture and decoration; upstairs, the **Museum of the Puerto Rican Family**, depicting life in San Juan a hundred years ago. Furniture, toys, music-boxes and nostalgia are on view here.

The statue of Columbus on Plaza de Colón was erected in 1893, on the 400th anniversary of his discovery of Puerto Rico.

South of the square, the social centre of 19th-century San Juan, the **Tapia Theatre**, was restored in 1976 at about 300 times its original cost. The 1832 building had been financed by contributions plus a one-cent tax on every loaf of bread. Again in use as an opera house and concert hall, the venerable theatre gets its name from the Puerto Rican playwright Alejandro Tapia y Rivera (1826–82).

Fort San Cristobal

A relatively modern element in San Juan's defence system, it was completed in 1783 and is one of the largest Spanish fortifications in the Americas. Moats, ramps and tunnels link five separate units with the main part of the fort, looming far above the Atlantic. The National Park Service conducts tours or you can wander around on your own.

El Morro

At the peninsula's tip, El Morro is San Juan's most impressive fort. You can look around at your leisure or take one of the tours run by the National Park Service. Within the seemingly impregnable stone bulwark of the fort, you will find gentle expanses of grass, even a golf course (though it's no longer in use).

You'll marvel at the engineering work that went into this self-contained, six-storey city. Walk down the tunnels, stairways, ramps and parade grounds; visit the ammunition stores, cannons, dungeons and kitchens. Often besieged, El Morro fell only once —to the British in 1598. But, on that occasion, the invaders had rolled in from the rear over an easy beachhead, where the Condado hotels rise today.

Metropolitan Area

The tourist track to and from the old city passes through the area called Puerta de Tierra (Land Gateway). In transit have a look at Puerto Rico's El Capitolio, a neoclassical building resembling the US Capitol in Washington. Another 20th-century landmark, the Caribe Hilton Hotel, was built during "Operation Bootstrap", a plan devised by the government during the Depression and World War II to transform the island from an underdeveloped backwater to a pace-setting industrial society. On the seafront alongside the hotel, the smallest of San Juan's 18th-century forts protected the eastern approach to the old city. Fort San Jerónimo now includes a Museum of Military History with old swords and flintlocks and a pre-1898 collection of Spanish uniforms.

Just to the east begins the Condado section, sometimes called the Miami Beach of Puerto Rico.

Claude Hervé-Bazin

istockphoto.com/Rodriguez

Huber/Gräfenhain

Music has always been an important part of Puerto Rican culture. | A colourful street in Old San Juan. | Isla Verde Beach curves along the modern district of San Juan.

The rainforest of El Yunque shelters a great variety of flora and fauna.

iStockphoto.com/Koluvzija

En la Isla

En la isla—"Out on the island"—is what the Puerto Ricans call everything beyond the sprawl of metropolitan San Juan. The change of pace from the bustling commercial centre is sudden and therapeutic. Drive half an hour from the capital and you can find yourself in utter wilderness. Two of the most popular outings from San Juan—El Yunque rain forest and Luquillo Beach—are often combined in one tour.

El Yunque

As you'll soon discover, a tropical rain forest is just that: steaming hot, dripping wet, dense jungle. El Yunque (The Anvil), named after one of its prominent mountains, covers 11,200 ha (28,000 acres) and comprises a bird and wildlife sanctuary operated by the US Forest Service. Even if you escape the average of five daily showers, you'll be impressed to learn that more than 100 billion gallons of water drench these tangled slopes every year. There are several well-maintained hiking trails, ranging from a 15-minute stroll to a trek to the peak of El Yunque, at 1,065 m (3,500 ft).

About 240 species of trees grow here, all indigenous. Watch for the stout, gnarled Colorado trees. One well-known specimen is estimated to be 2,500 years old. You'll also see hundreds of intertwined woody liana vines, towering Sierra palms with white-blossomed fruit spikes and frond-topped tree ferns. Seek out tiny orchids and asuséna, a long white tuberose which exudes a glorious perfume—but only at night—and listen for the song of the *coquí* frog, Puerto Rico's unofficial emblem.

Luquillo Beach

Near the turnoff for El Yunque, Luquillo, with its attractive seaside coconut grove and colourful snack stalls, is the best known of the public beaches *(balnearios)*.

Fajardo

At the eastern tip of the island, Fajardo has a huge marina, Puerto del Rey, and several beaches with calm, clear waters. Nearby headlands, **Las Cabezas de San Juan**, form a natural reserve of coral reefs, lagoons, mangroves and forest. Ferries take you to the peaceful, hilly island of Vieques and unspoilt Culebra, whose coral reefs offer fantastic snorkelling and diving.

Ponce

Also known as the Pearl of the South, Ponce is Puerto Rico's second city, a gem of preserved colonial architecture centering on the stately cathedral of Our Lady of Guadalupe, on Plaza

istockphoto.com/Rodriguez

istockphoto.com/Hanke

Las Delicias. The cultural highlight of the town is the excellent **Museum of Art**, with a fine collection of European and American art from the 3rd century BC to the present day. There is also a small display of pre-Columbian ceramics, and one of Art Nouveau glass. To the north, the **Cruceta el Vigia** is a plexiglass cross-shaped lookout affording a splendid ocean view.

Tibes Indian Ceremonial Center

This reconstructed Arawak village north of Ponce can be visited on a guided tour. It was discovered by chance after a hurricane in 1975 when pieces of bones, shells and ceramic fragments were uncovered by the torrential rains. Excavations revealed a large ceremonial complex complete with nine ball courts and three plazas, one of them star-shaped. There is also a cemetery with 186 skeletons from the Igneri culture (from AD 400 to 600) and other pre-Taino tribes. The Taino Indians repopulated the abandoned site around AD 1000.

Claude Hervé-Bazin

istockphoto.com/Gonzalez

The beautiful flamboyant Royal Poinciana tree *(Delonix regia).* | A cocky little *coquí* in the rainforest. | Plaza las Delicias in Ponce. | An Indian face sculpted into the mountainside.

San Germán

In the southwest, the island's second-oldest city, founded in 1511, is a peaceful, picturesque town that has retained its Spanish colonial atmosphere. On one of its two plazas, the Gothic-style **Porta Coéli Church** (Gate of Heaven) dates from 1606, when it was built by Dominican monks. It has been restored to serve as a museum of religious art, including Mexican colonial paintings and wood statuary of the 18th and 19th centuries. A music festival is held in the town each summer.

Nearby beaches include **Phosphorescent Bay** and the delightful **Boquerón**, great for swimming.

Mayagüez

Centered on the Spanish-style Plaza Colon, the town has superb **botanical gardens** (the Tropical Agricultural Research Station at the university) and the **Dr Juan A. Rivero Zoo**. It stands at one end of the **Panoramic Route** which runs the whole length of the island, through the Cordillera Central all the way to Yabucoa. Its narrow roads meander through forest reserves and green valleys, offering magnificent views.

Mona Island

By chartered boat or plane from Mayagüez, you can reach tiny Mona, called the Galapagos of the Caribbean. Taino Indians lived here, then pirates and privateers, but now it is left to the wildlife. No more than 100 visitors are allowed at a time to see the giant iguanas, the hawksbill and leatherback turtles, the red-footed boobies and other seabirds.

Rincón

At the westernmost point of the islands, the mountains run down to the sea, and the lovely beaches are holiday favourites with Puerto Rican families and American surfers.

Humpback whales visit these waters in winter, and platforms for spotting whales and dolphins have been built near El Faro, the lighthouse.

Río Camuy

More than a million years ago, the Camuy River carved out great subterranean caverns from the limestone of this jagged karst region in the northwest of the island, a paradise for spelunkers. **Río Camuy Cave Park** has civilized the whole area, with picnic areas, walking trails, exhibition hall and souvenir shop. Safe viewing of the underground world is organized at Cueva Clara, where visitors ride a sort of tram into a sinkhole to admire the impressive formations of stalagtites and stalagmites.

THE HARD FACTS

Airport. Luís Muñoz Marin (SJU) airport is 14 km (9 miles) southeast of San Juan. Buses and taxis take 20 to 30 minutes to reach the city centre.

Banks. Open Monday to Friday 8.30 or 9 a.m.–2.30 p.m.

Climate. Hot and tropical, varying little throughout the year. Temperatures average 27°C (80°F) in low elevations and 21°C (70°F) in the mountains. The rainy season stretches from April to November. About a quarter of the annual rainfall occurs during the hurricane season, which runs from June to November.

Clothing. Away from the beach, it's fairly conservative, but shorts are acceptable in most public places. At night, people tend to dress up, especially in the casinos and nightclubs, and jackets are often required for men in smart restaurants.

istockphoto.com/Pershern

Communications. San Juan (area code 1 787) is part of the US network. The international access code is 011. San Juan and most numbers in Puerto Rico start with 1 787. The big hotels have Internet access, and you will find Internet cafés in the cities.

Customs Allowance. Visitors of 21 years or older may import, duty-free: 200 cigarettes or 50 cigars or 2 kg (4.4 lb) tobacco and 1 quart of alcoholic beverages.

Driving. Traffic drives on the right. Car hire is available at the airport and at city agencies.

Electricity. 110 volts AC, 60 Hz.

Holidays. January 1, New Year's Day; January 6, Epiphany; 2nd Monday in January, Birthday of Eugenio María de Hostos; 3rd Monday in January, Martin Luther King Day; 3rd Monday in February, President's Day; March 22, Emancipation of the Slaves; 3rd Monday in April, José de Diego's Birthday; March–April, Good

Friday; last Monday in May, Memorial Day; July 4, US Independence Day; 3rd Monday in July, Luis Muñoz Rivera's Birthday; July 25, Constitution Day; July 27 José Celso Barbosa's Birthday; 1st Monday in September, Labour Day; 2nd Monday in October, Columbus Day; November 11, Veterans' Day; November 19, Discovery of Puerto Rico Day; 4th Thursday in November, Thanksgiving; December 24, Christmas Eve (often half-day); December 25, Christmas Day; December 31, New Year's Eve (often half-day).

Language. Puerto Ricans consider Spanish to be their mother tongue. In San Juan, many people speak English as well.

Money. US dollars are the official currency, sometimes referred to as the peso. Some establishments will accept Canadian dollars. Major credit cards are widely accepted.

Shops. Most shops are open Monday to Saturday 9 a.m.–7 p.m., Thursday and Friday 9 a.m.–9 p.m. On Sunday the shopping malls open 11 a.m.–5 p.m.

Time. GMT –4, all year round.

Tipping. Taxi drivers expect a 15 per cent tip. Major restaurants and nightclubs automatically add a service charge to the bill, but inexpensive restaurants do not normally do so: in such cases you can add 15 to 20 per cent for good service.

Transport. Local bus services (*guaguas*) run between the capital and main towns, but they stop around 9 p.m. Taxis include *linea*, which pick up and drop off passengers wherever they wish and have fixed rates; *tourist taxis* which charge set rates for travel between the airport and major tourist sites; *publicos* (share-taxis) which operate during daylight hours on regular, fixed routes. Ordinary taxis are hired by the hour. Charges are metered except on charter trips outside the usual zones. You can hail them in the street or call them by phone. There is a rapid transit train, *Tren Urbano*, in San Juan linking the central business district to residential and employment areas; some of the stations are underground. It is planned to expand the system.

Water. Tap water is purified and considered safe to drink but you may prefer bottled mineral water. Do not swim or paddle in rivers and streams.

A chaos of rocks forms a dramatic back-
ground to The Baths, a famous cove on
Virgin Gorda.

hemis.fr/Torrione

VIRGIN ISLANDS

This cluster of islands, islets and shrub-swathed rocks has been collectively called the Virgins since Columbus sailed through. Because they were so beautiful and numerous, he named them after St Ursula's 11,000 martyred maidens of Christian belief. Rising out of a crystal-blue sea, they're surprisingly green and hilly. In all there are some 80 islands, owned by the United States or Britain. Most of them are tiny and inhabited only by lucky birds, and the majority are verdant and volcanic. All form part of the extended arc of islands known as the Lesser Antilles, which haphazardly define where the Atlantic ends and the Caribbean begins.

British Virgin Islands

Few people can tell you for sure how many islands make up the British Virgins—it all depends on the tide. There are in fact around 60 islands and cays, of which 16 are inhabited. Mostly of volcanic origin, these tiny and almost forgotten islands, the BVI as they are known locally, are a sleepy relic of an empire. British rule rests lightly on the 23,500 inhabitants whose dignity and independent outlook stem from a long tradition of land ownership. They will greet you with overwhelming charm—even if their dialect of English might baffle you at first.

Tortola

Almost 80 per cent of the population lives on Tortola, the best-known and largest of the BVI. The name is Spanish for turtle-dove.

Road Town

The capital of the BVI has no pretensions. Main Street winds through town, and a waterfront drive connects the old town to **Wickhams Cay**. Many banks and other financial institutions are located on this land which was formerly a burial ground for slaves. As befits any colonial capital, Road Town also has a Government House and Legislative Assembly building.

BRITISH VIRGINS FLASHBACK

Pre-Columbian era
The first known settlers of the islands are the Ciboney Indians from the South American mainland. They are followed by the Arawak Indians who in turn succumb to the warlike Caribs.

15th–16th centuries
Columbus meets a hostile reception when he tries to land on the islands during his second voyage in 1493. He names them Las Once Mil Vírgines and claims them for Spain. Spanish slave-hunters and pirates wipe out the Indians.

17th century
Dutch buccaneers build a settlement and fort on Tortola in 1648. The British seize Tortola and annex the islands in 1672. Settlers establish cotton, sugar and indigo plantations on Tortola and Virgin Gorda.

18th–19th centuries
The first half of the 18th century sees increasing prosperity and the arrival of missionaries—notably Quakers. The seat of government is transferred from Virgin Gorda to Tortola in 1741, and in 1774 the first elected assembly meets. The American War of Independence marks the start of economic decline. By the end of the century, law and order are reported to have broken down. The Napoleonic Wars bring British war-ships to Road Harbour which becomes a free port, but the economic decline is accelerated by drought and a disastrous hurricane. The islands become part of the Leeward Island Federation in 1816. In 1834 the islands' 5,000 slaves are freed. A revolt breaks out in 1853, and cholera sweeps the islands. Plantations are abandoned and the islands revert to bush.

20th century–present
The colonial government makes an attempt to revive agriculture, but two hurricanes in 1916 and 1924 spell economic setback. The British Virgin Islands become a separate colony in 1956. A constitution in 1967 gives the islands a ministerial system of government and they are now largely self-governing, with the Premier as head of government as decreed by a new constitution in 2007. Tourism and offshore banking have emerged as major industries.

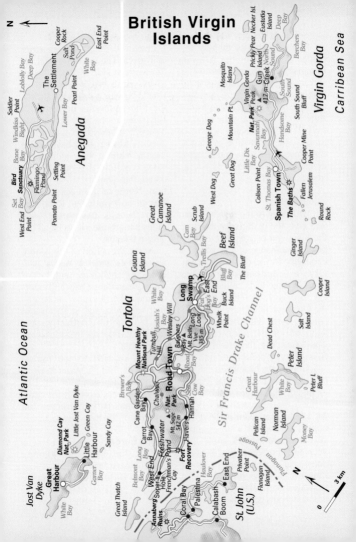

Look in at the tiny **Folk Museum** on Main Street. Its display includes artefacts of the Arawak Indians and of the plantation and slavery eras, photographs of local history and architecture, and bits and pieces salvaged from the shipwrecks that strew the islands.

If all this sightseeing is just too much, cool off awhile in the **J.R. O'Neal Botanical Garden** in the centre of town, in the shade of exotic tropical foliage.

Island Sights

On your way to the beaches you will pass the overgrown ruins of the big sugar estates that used to be the mainstay of the island's economy in the early 19th century. In better condition are the ruins of three forts called Recovery, Shirley and Charlotte, and the Dungeon at Havers, all on the south shore. The best bathing spots are on the north coast. At **Cane Garden Bay**, the beach slopes from leaning palm trees into the sea. Behind the beach you can see one local industry that hasn't changed much in three centuries—the rum distillery. Visit for a tasting and admire the grand copper boiling vat, a huge copper still made by slaves some 200 years ago. Further down the north coast, at **Carrot Bay**, a shell museum displays not only these treasures from the sea but also wooden boats and other crafts.

Hills

Scenery is the high point of a tour of Tortola. The top of **Joe's Hill**, on the western side of Road Town, gives you a bird's-eye view of Road Harbour. **Soldier's Hill** affords the fine panorama of Brewer's Bay, where forested hills enclose a superb snorkelling and bathing beach. Above the bay, **Mount Healthy National Park** includes a stone windmill that once turned on an 18th-century sugar plantation. North of the Cane Garden Bay turnoff on Ridge Road, the **Briercliffe-Davis Observatory** provides panoramic views of all the Virgin Islands.

At the West End of the island, **Soper's Hole Wharf & Marina** is a charming anchorage with lots of shops, restaurants, bars and entertainment. Ferries run from here to Jost Van Dyke and St Thomas in the US Virgins. Attractive terraced villas dot the hillsides amid the foliage.

Walk or ride to the top of 542-m (1,780-ft) **Mount Sage** to see what the island looked like before slaves cleared it for cane. A national park preserves the remains of the lush forest.

Virgin Gorda

During the half-hour journey you'll have a spectacular view of parts of Tortola inaccessible by road, as well as of the islands west of Virgin Gorda. This is the third-largest of the British Virgin Islands. Only 3,000 people live here, and it's hard to believe that it was once a thriving commercial centre.

The capital is **Spanish Town**, a quaint settlement with shops, restaurants and tiny hotels. South of the yacht harbour, stone walls remain from an old Spanish fort in the **Little Fort National Park**, and on the island's southwest tip, you can see relics of a copper mine worked by Cornish miners in the middle of the 19th century. But this island is best known for **The Baths**, about a mile down Millionaire's Road from the town. It's as if a giant hand has flung huge, house-sized granite boulders across the white sand of a cove. The sea rushes in to form a labyrinth of crystal-clear channels and pools, which shimmer in the reflected light.

Other Islands

To the southwest of Virgin Gorda stretches a string of cays.

Peter Island

Directly opposite Road Town across the Sir Francis Drake Channel, Peter Island is a luxurious, privately owned resort. The port is **Sprat Bay**, popular with yachtsmen from around the world. The sweeping crescent of **Deadman's Bay** is rated as one of the world's most romantic beaches, and there are 30 dive sites, notably Carrot Shoal and Shark Point.

Norman Island

It is said to be Robert Louis Stevenson's Treasure Island. You'll enjoy snorkelling and exploring the sea caves at **Treasure Point**. Close by is the rock Dead Chest Island celebrated in the song "Fifteen men on a dead man's chest, yo-ho-ho and a bottle of rum". It's an uninhabited national park with three dive sites, including the magnificent **Painted Walls**: vertical rock faces encrusted with brightly coloured sponges and cup corals.

Salt Island

Beyond Dead Chest, this island used to provide the English monarch with an annual sack of salt from its ponds. Divers come to explore the extensive wreck of *RMS Rhone*, a transatlantic Royal Mail steamer smashed against a reef by a hurricane in 1867.

Jost Van Dyke and Anegada

Northwest of Tortola, Jost Van Dyke's Great Harbour is a pretty village of wooden houses that seems lost in time, while limestone and coral Anegada, with its infinite white sand beaches, is as far away from it all as you can get. The main town is called The Settlement.

Plain sailing over the deep blue waters of
the Caribbean in the Virgin Islands.

istockphoto.com /De Mattos

US Virgin Islands

The majority of Virgin Islanders are descendants of African slaves who laboured for European plantation owners until emancipation in the mid-19th century. More and more of the population, however, is not native-born: "down islanders" from elsewhere in the Caribbean, as well as Puerto Ricans and mainland Americans have been moving in to these still sparsely inhabited islands, particularly St Thomas and St Croix. The resulting ethnic and cultural blend is intriguing, and unusually harmonious.

St Thomas

The busiest and best-known of the Virgin Islands is St Thomas, which enjoys its reputation of being a shoppers' paradise. But retail therapy is only one of the many pleasures which it has to offer. Exploring the island, with its dramatic wooded hills, intimate beaches, historic houses and inspiring seascapes, is another. The capital and only city of St Thomas is the prettily named Charlotte Amalie, honouring the consort of Christian V, king of Denmark in the 17th century. Most of the island's population lives in the town, which rises steeply and majestically from the port district. The port is the starting and finishing point for many cruises; there is always a line of ships at the quayside.

Charlotte Amalie

The Virgin Islands Legislature, a 15-member Senate, occupies the stately building just beyond the Coast Guard headquarters at King's Wharf. It was built over a century ago to house Danish police, and is where the Danish flag was lowered for the last time when the US formally took possession of the Virgin Islands in 1917.

Across the road, a solid chunk of history is embodied in an aloof fortress with the date 1671 on its façade. Actually, the date of its construction is uncertain. Today the dungeon of **Fort Christian** serves as the local museum. Exhibits of old navigational charts, African ornaments, Stone Age Indian tools found on the island and a collection of rare Caribbean seashells are set up in the former cells.

Frederick Lutheran Church, thought to be the island's oldest, was built in 1826 to replace an 18th-century church destroyed in a fire. A wide staircase leads to an imposing entrance. Further east along the same street (Norre Gade), the **Moravian Memorial Church** with its fine wooden cupola dates from 1882.

Government House, a gracious, three-storey brick edifice, with long balconies in wrought iron, was built by the Danish rulers in 1867, and a red sentry box stand-

US VIRGINS FLASHBACK

15th–16th centuries
After Columbus claims the islands for Spain, the Indian inhabitants are forced into slavery. The islands become the haunt of pirates.

17th century
In 1625, English and Dutch settlers establish rival outposts on St Croix. After 20 years of bloody struggle, the English prevail, but they are expelled by Spanish forces in 1650, who themselves surrender to the French in the same year. St Croix is bequeathed in 1653 to the Knights of Malta, who sell out to the French West India Company 12 years later. In 1657 Dutch settlers establish a colony on St Thomas but soon abandon the island. A contingent of Danes and Norwegians found the settlement of Charlotte Amalie in 1672.

18th century
Danish settlers from St Thomas cross to St John in 1717, establishing plantations of cotton and tobacco. St Thomas is declared a free port in 1724. A slave uprising on St John in 1733 gives the slaves a free community for six months. Forces are brought in to quell the rebellion and all the slaves die, many committing suicide at Mary's Point. The same year, France sells St Croix to the Danish West India Company. Denmark names St Thomas a crown colony in 1734.

19th century
St Thomas and St John change hands several times while the English and the Danes struggle to establish supremacy. The economy of St Thomas declines in the 1820s with a slump in cane sugar prices and the advent of the steamship. Governor von Scholten frees the slaves of the Danish islands in 1848. Cholera epidemics sweep the Virgins. Riots break out and sugar production all but ceases.

20th century–present
During World War I, the US buys St Thomas and St John, together with St Croix and some 50 islets and outcrops for $25 million. Islanders are granted voting rights in 1936. They gain greater independence in 1954 with the creation of a three-branch central government, headed since 1970 by an elected governor.

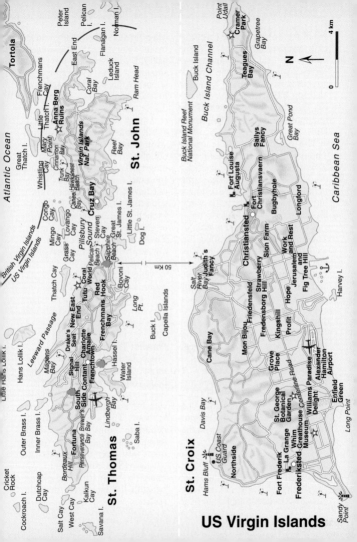

US Virgin Islands

ing at the bottom of the ceremonial stairs reminds us of their presence. The mansion now serves as the office of the elected governor of the Virgin Islands. Visiting VIPs are received here, too, but the governor now resides in a mansion on top of Denmark Hill.

The higher you climb in St Thomas the more thrilling the views. This is where the well-to-do 18th-century colonists built their houses on hilltops overlooking the harbour. The hills were too steep for roads, so stone staircases were built as step-streets. The most famous is called the **99 Steps**, at the top of which is **Blackbeard's Castle** or Skytsborg, a stone tower with a superb view, and now a hotel. It was the haunt of a legendary 18th-century buccaneer, Bristol-born Edward Teach.

A historical highlight of the island is the **St Thomas Synagogue**, rebuilt in 1833 on the site of several previous Jewish temples. A French architect laid out this traditional design, with three sides of benches facing inward. The sand on the floor is thought to commemorate the exodus of the Jews from Egypt.

Shopping District

Downhill from the synagogue, the shopping district of Charlotte Amalie is concentrated on or near Main Street (still officially known by its Danish name, **Dronningens Gade**). By any standard, this is a shopper's dream come true. Few streets in the world sell so many luxurious goods so temptingly displayed.

Amidst the carefully re-modelled Danish warehouses filled with a multitude of duty-free delights, the building at 14 Dronningens Gade provides an artistic footnote: this was the birthplace of Camille Pissarro (1830–1903), sometimes called the Father of French Impressionism. Though he lived most of his life in France, Pissarro was a Thomian and always maintained his Danish citizenship.

Main Street becomes less glamorous—but no less fascinating—at **Market Square**, where islanders buy and sell local fruits and vegetables.

Paradise Point

The point is the site of the large, modern **Havensight Mall**. From here you can take a "gondola" that whisks you up the mountainside for a sweeping view of the harbour. The mall is also the departure point of the 2-hour **Atlantis Submarine** trip. A tender takes you over to Buck Island (just off St Croix), where you board the submarine and plunge beneath the ocean to view the reef.

Hassel Island

A narrow, shallow isthmus used to link Hassel Island to the "mainland". When the United States bought the Virgins, the navy quickly dredged a major channel to separate Hassel from St Thomas, thus providing the American fleet an alternative escape route in case the harbour should be attacked. Among Hassel Island's landmarks is a mountaintop fort built in the 19th century as a signal tower.

Frenchtown

Almost attached to Hassel Island, the area acquired its name from the French-speaking settlers who came from the French Caribbean colony of St Barthélemy in the mid-19th century. They have retained their ancient Norman dialect—and their fishing skills.

Brewer's Bay

The charming white-sand beach is owned by the University of the Virgin Islands but open to the public. The college occupies 70 ha (175 acres) of attractively landscaped hillsides.

Mountain Top

Nearly 460 m (1,500 ft) high, Mountain Top affords a magnificent view down onto Magens Bay and out to an array of US off-islands and the British Virgins. The famous banana daiquiri was invented in the original hotel standing at this spot, destroyed by a hurricane. You can still sample the traditional cocktail here.

Drake's Seat

Legend says that Sir Francis Drake sat here in 1595, while he surveyed the fleet he had assembled to attack Puerto Rico. By that moment in his career, the most famous of Elizabethan admirals had captured many Spanish bastions. But the tactics he devised on this hill failed to match the firepower of El Morro fortress defending San Juan. Embittered and feverish, the navigator died soon after this defeat and was buried at sea off Panama.

Beaches

Magens Bay is the island's biggest and most flawless beach. The

---

Blackbeard The Buccaneer.
Edward Teach is said to have accumulated 14 wives, though it's uncertain whether they were wed consecutively or rather deployed concurrently on various islands. The scandalous career of this giant among scoundrels ended in a shoot-out with the British navy in 1718. Blackbeard's tower achieved sudden respectability in 1831 when it was converted to an astronomical observatory.

palm-backed stretch of sand, unspoiled thanks to government conservation efforts, really is one of the most glorious beaches in the world. Arthur S. Fairchild, an American publishing tycoon, gave the property to the people of the Virgin Islands in 1946.

More of the best beaches are just downhill from the Smith Bay road heading to the east end of the island. At **Coki Beach**, Coral World, an underwater observation tower right on the sea bed, gives insight into the habitat and inhabitants of the marine world—exotic fish, coral formations, deep-water flowers and so on. Coki is also rated the best local beach for snorkelling. Luxury hotels and condominiums snuggle on secluded coves with names as appealing as Pineapple Beach, Pelican Bay and Sapphire Beach.

Bluebeard's Castle

This round stone tower of brick and rubble masonry was built by the Danish government in 1678 as a coast defense installation. Its 11 cannon were manned until 1735. According to local legend, Bluebeard used this tower as a lookout, lair and love-nest. One version recounts that the pirate discovered his bride there with another man; he slew her and sailed away, never to be heard of again. In fact, no official record of Bluebeard's tenancy exists. But it adds a piquant touch to what is now the honeymoon suite of a luxury hotel, built around the tower in 1933.

St John

On the smallest and most beautiful of the three major American islands, nature reigns supreme. The intrusion of humans is minimal, and the result is the envy of the Caribbean. There are forty coves enclosing a hundred hues of blue and green and semi-circular beaches of powdery white coral sand. Behind them are coconut groves and then tangled forests with ruins of old Danish plantations. Flowers, ferns and butterflies abound.

St John owes its unspoiled tranquillity to the fact that 56 per cent of its rugged landscape and most of its offshore waters are preserved as the **Virgin Islands National Park**. This park has existed since 1956 on acreage donated by Laurance Rockefeller, but it has since been extended to incorporate Hassel Island on St Thomas. There are more than 20 hiking trails, along with guided tours and historic programmes. Be sure to pick up maps and information at the Visitor's Center, on the north side of the harbour.

Cruz Bay

The sleepy capital of St John is so tiny that no one has even bothered to name its streets. The harbour, also called Cruz Bay, is used by yachts and the ferries from St Thomas. Modern life has made some inroads—even here there are now shopping malls: Mongoose Junction and Wharfside Village.

From high on Centerline Road which climbs up around the tallest peak, Bordeaux Mountain, 389 m (1,277 ft), there are truly breathtaking views of the Atlantic, Caribbean and nearby islands. You'll see down to remote Mary's Point on the north shore where St John's slave rebellion of 1733 ended tragically. It's also known as Suicide Point.

From another lookout you can see as far as St Croix on a clear day across the 65 km (40 miles) of water.

From **Coral Bay Overlook**, no less than eleven of the neighbouring British Virgin Islands lining the channel named for Sir Francis Drake make a photograph to remember. From here you can gaze down on **St John's Hurricane Hole**, a protected bay where sailors have fled storms over the centuries. This panorama is considered by many to be the best in the Caribbean.

Towering above the picturesque north shore ruins of the **Annaberg** sugar and rum factory is a 150-year-old windmill, one of the largest in the Virgin Islands.

Françoise Ohayon

Trunk Bay on St John has all the ingredients required to make the ideal beach.

Beaches

No picture book can prepare you for the glorious beaches strung one after another along St John's reef-fringed northwestern shore.

Trunk Bay, endlessly praised and photographed, may well be the most perfect of perfect beaches. The snorkelling trail in the emerald water is ideal for novices. Its sunken symbols and signs are clearly visible at a maximum depth of 4 m (13 ft).

Whenever Greta Garbo wanted to be alone, she checked in to **Caneel Bay**, a resort founded by Laurance Rockefeller. Celebrities, politicians and industrialists appreciate its gentle beaches and unobtrusive luxury. The resort itself is one of St John's tourist sights. Ordinary mortals may stroll the grounds, examine the beaches of fine sand, buy a drink or have lunch. There are some interesting old sugar buildings.

St Croix

Long, leisurely and lovely, St Croix lies in the Caribbean some 40 miles (64 km) south of the other Virgin Islands. The name is pronounced Saint Croy; it means "Holy Cross". You'll soon appreciate that this is a very special tropical island. The unhurried Crucians number about 54,000 and live on St Croix's 212 sq km (82 sq miles) of rolling countryside and satellite isles. That makes it by far the largest of the Virgins, but boasting is not the style. There are only two towns, Frederiksted and Christiansted.

Frederiksted

Fronting on the tranquil west-coast sea, Frederiksted wears a sleepy look, and its few modern buildings don't even begin to disturb the old-fashioned, world-passed-by atmosphere.

A vital feature is the new pier put up in 1994 to accommodate several cruise ships at once. The nearby **Aquarium** blossomed out then, too, adding more tanks and what they call a "touch pond" where you can make close acquaintance with friendly denizens of the sea.

Fort Frederik, now restored, stands near the pier; it was built in the mid-18th century, primarily to discourage smuggling which flourished from the west end of St Croix. As unlikely as insurrection seems here now, it was at this fort that harried Governor von Scholten declared, in an explosive situation in 1848: "All unfree in the Danish West Indies are from today free".

Strolling Frederiksted's esplanade and handful of downtown streets, you'll notice an odd architectural mixture nicknamed "Victorian gingerbread". When local leaders went on a rampage in the labour riots of 1878, the upper levels of the buildings were destroyed in the blaze, but the Danish stone bases survived.

The mid-18th-century outdoor produce market is open some mornings, but an even better show is the seaside fish market which also began life when Frederiksted did.

Around the Island

Leaving Frederiksted, a pleasant little coastal road runs north, meandering through the dense foliage of St Croix's small rain forest and on to the Virgin Islands' celebrated Carambola Golf Course.

Elsewhere on the north shore, marking the site where Columbus's crew came ashore on his second voyage, the **Salt River Bay National Historical Park** harbours a wide variety of endangered flora and fauna.

A main highway, Centerline Road, crosses the island, to link the two towns. Near its western end is St Croix's proudest land-bound attraction, **Whim Greathouse**. You'll want to spend at least an hour on this elegant estate with its great house built by an eccentric Danish planter in 1794. A fascinating 1832 apothecary shop has been recreated, and the huge stone windmill and mule mill, both used to grind sugar, have been fully restored.

Farther east is **St George Botanical Garden,** set around the ruins of another Afro-Danish sugar cane plantation.

Christiansted

A small wedge of Christiansted, beginning at King's Wharf, was the heart of the Danish capital. It's preserved as a historic site by the US National Park Service.

Fort Christiansvaern, overlooking the harbour, manages to appear formidable, though it was never fired on. The guns on the parapet are unused, and the view over Gallows Bay is superb. Dating back to 1734, the neat yellow fort is the oldest structure on the island, though greatly restored.

Leaving the fort through the sally port, you'll spy a steeple straight ahead at the edge of town. The **Steeple Building** was the island's first Danish Lutheran church. Military, medical, municipal and educational functions followed over the years. Today,

beneath the steeple which dates back to 1795, the edifice is an instant museum of the Danish West Indies. Apart from displays of the history of sugar and rum, aboriginal Indian artefacts show how the Caribs and Arawaks cooked, fished and hunted.

Government House on King Street has a narrow ballroom where the Danish elite drank and danced away the long colonial evenings. Not only governors but wealthy planter-merchants lived at times in this admired residence, part of which stood as early as 1747. The red wooden sentry box dates back to the Danish period.

Buck Island

Any morning at the Christiansted wharf, take your choice of sloop, schooner, catamaran or glass-bottomed boat for the 9-km (5.5-mile) trip to Buck Island off St Croix's northeastern shore. With its fabulous underwater trail through an encircling coral reef, the island was proclaimed a US National Monument by President John F. Kennedy in 1961. Boat skippers provide masks and fins, and there are various raft-glass viewing devices so that no one need miss the fish. You'll be guided along the natural trail, which has sunken arrows and signs identifying coral species perfectly visible in water no more than 4 m (13 ft) deep.

THE HARD FACTS

Airports. Lettsome (EIS) on Beef Island is 14 km (9 miles) from Road Town on Tortola. Virgin Gorda (VIJ) is 3 km (2 miles) from Spanish Town. Anegada also has an airport. St Thomas (STT) is 3 km (2 miles) from Charlotte Amalie, and St Croix (STX) 18 km (10 miles) from Christiansted.

Banks. BVI banks open Monday to Friday 9 a.m.–2 p.m. (some to 3 or 4 p.m.). USVI banks open Monday to Thursday 9 a.m.–2.30 p.m.; Friday 9 a.m.–2 p.m. and 3.30–5 p.m.

Climate. Thanks to the steadily soothing trade winds, the Virgin Islands boast fairly of the best weather in the West Indies; lower humidity than elsewhere and an average annual temperature of 77°F (25°C). Rare is the day without predominantly blue sky and sunshine. The hurricane season is from June to November.

Clothing. Dress is generally informal, but beachwear should be kept only for the beach. Take tropical, lightweight clothing.

Communications. The international country code for BVI is 1 284 49 and for USVI 1 340. The international dialling code from BVI is 00, from USVI 001. The major hotels provide Internet access, and you will also find Internet cafés in the towns.

Customs Allowance. BVI: free import by passengers of 18 years and over of 200 cigarettes or 50 cigars or 225 g tobacco; 1 quart of wine or spirits. USVI: visitors over 21 may import duty-free 200 cigarettes or 100 cigars or 2 kg of tobacco; otherwise duty must be paid on all imported gifts and alcohol.

Driving. Driving is on the left. The maximum speed limit on BVI is 64 kph (40 mph); on USVI 35 kph (20 mph) in

istockphoto.com/Mahler

towns and 55 kph (35 mph) elsewhere. National licences are accepted in USVI but to hire a car on BVI you will need a temporary BVI licence, issued on production of a current foreign licence.

Electricity. BVI: 110 volts AC, 60 Hz, with sockets for 2-pin (flat) plugs. USVI: 120 volts AC, 60 Hz.

Holidays. *All islands*: January 1, New Year's Day; March–April, Good Friday, Easter Monday; December 25–26, Christmas.

BVI: March, Lavity Stoutt's Birthday, Commonwealth Day; June, Whit Monday, 2nd Saturday, Queen's Birthday; July 1, Territory Day; 1st Monday, Tuesday and Wednesday in August, festival days; October 21, St Ursula's Day.

USVI: January 6, Three Kings' Day, 3rd Monday in January, Martin Luther King Day; February, Presidents' Day; March 31, Transfer Day; March–April, Holy Thursday; July 3 Danish West Indies Emancipation Day; May, Memorial Day; June, Organic Act Day; July 4, US Independence Day; July, Hurricane Supplication Day; September, Labor Day; October, Columbus Day, Puerto Rico Friendship Day, Virgin Islands Thanksgiving Day; November 1, D. Hamilton Jackson Day; November, Veterans' Day, US Thanksgiving Day.

Language. English. Spanish and Creole are widely spoken in the US Virgin Islands.

Money. The official currency is the US dollar. The main credit cards and travellers cheques, preferably in US$, are widely accepted.

Time. GMT–4, all year round.

Tipping. Hotels automatically add a 10–12 per cent service charge.

Transport. Taxis cover standard journeys at fixed rates. They can also be hired on an hourly or daily basis. The drivers are excellent guides. A public bus service operates on St Thomas from Charlotte Amalie to Red Hook and Bordeaux.

Water. Town supplies are drinkable; bottled mineral water is available.

Shaping the dough for French-style baguettes on La Désirade.

Hemis.fr / Du Boisberranger

FRENCH WEST INDIES

Guadeloupe, the largest of the French West Indies, spreads its wings midway along the Lesser Antilles chain. Columbus named it after a Spanish monastery, but the Carib Indians living there called it Karukera, Island of Beautiful Waters. Today its unspoiled charm complements the sophistication of Martinique, the other main French island 160 km (100 miles) to the south, between English-speaking Dominica and Saint Lucia. Guadeloupe's administrative dependencies are Les Saintes, Marie-Galante and Désirade. Saint-Martin and Saint-Barthélemy are now French Overseas Collectivities.

Guadeloupe

The island we know as Guadeloupe is in fact made up of two separate isles linked by a drawbridge across a salt-water channel, the Rivière Salée (Salt River). On a map, it resembles a butterfly. The component islands are notably dissimilar; Grande-Terre is the smaller, drier and flatter of the two. It is the site of Pointe-à-Pitre, the commercial centre and largest city. The administrative capital, Basse-Terre, is located on the other island, also called Basse-Terre — literally Low Land — nestling at the foot of the famous Soufrière volcano.

Pointe-à-Pitre

A tiny fishing village three centuries ago, this city is named after a Dutchman, Pieter, said to have been the most popular fishmonger on the waterfront. Today, weathered banana boats chug past yachts and passenger liners in this lively tropical port. Don't miss the open-air market close by the wharves. Colourful mounds of fruit and vegetables lie heaped beside land crabs, dried fish, spices and nuts. The vendors, wearing straw hats or brightly patterned Madras handkerchiefs, will attempt to sell you almost anything from a piglet to a "spiritual spray" for your home.

FRENCH WEST INDIES FLASHBACK

Pre-Columbian era

Indians from the Orinoco basin in South America migrate up the Antilles chain, reaching Martinique and Guadeloupe by AD 200. They are followed by the Arawaks, another wave of Amerindians from the Orinoco, who settle throughout the Caribbean by AD 300. Their tranquillity is shattered by the arrival of the Caribs, who drive the men off island after island and appropriate their women.

15th–17th centuries

Christopher Columbus discovers Guadeloupe and neighbouring islands in 1493 and Martinique in 1502. The French start colonizing the islands in 1635, but it takes them several years to prevail against the Caribs. Sugar-cropping begins booming in the 1640s and slaves are brought from Africa to work the plantations. The French stake a claim in Saint-Barthélemy in 1648 and send over a boatload of Huguenot settlers from Brittany and Normandy in 1674.

18th–19th centuries

Britain and France battle for domination of the Antilles. Britain conquers Guadeloupe in 1759 and holds it for four years, and occupies Martinique for eight years from 1794. In 1784 Louis XVI gives St Barthélemy to Sweden in exchange for duty-free trading rights in Gothenburg. In 1838, the philanthropist Victor Schoelcher, Martinique's greatest hero, succeeds in having a law passed in France abolishing slavery. Ten years later, the law is implemented, freeing 87,500 slaves in Guadeloupe and 72,000 in Martinique. Contract workers begin to arrive from India and Africa to replace slave labour on the plantations. France buys back St Barthélemy from Sweden in 1878 for 320,000 gold francs.

20th century–present

Mont Pelée in Martinique erupts devastatingly in 1902, leaving more than 30,000 dead. Guadeloupe and Martinique become *départements* of France in 1946. Later, under an administrative reshuffle, they are renamed *régions*, each with a *préfet* named in Paris. Tourism, sugar exports, rum and bananas provide the main sources of income.

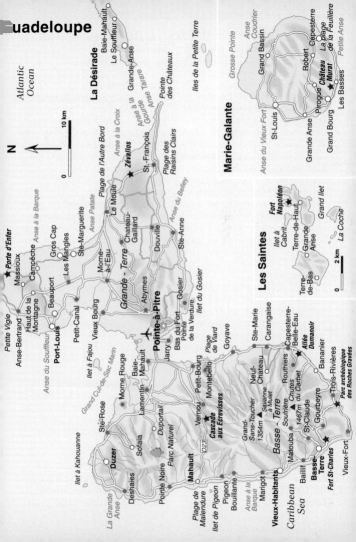

Place de la Victoire

In the heart of town, the café-lined square sprawls in the shade of royal palms and flame trees. The Victory of its name recalls the defeat of the English in 1795—when the governor Victor Hugues set up a guillotine here that made short work of some 4,000 white settlers. Just off the square, the 19th-century **Basilique Saint-Pierre et Saint-Paul** features unusual metal columns and balconies. Designed by a certain M. Trouille, it was destroyed three times by hurricane and restored each time. The stained-glass windows are the work of local artists.

Town Centre

Pointe-à-Pitre bustles by day and empties at night. Along Rue Frébault, the shops spill out over the pavement, and crowds of shoppers stroll up and down in front of the boutiques selling clothes and fabrics.

On the corner of Rue Peynier, the **Saint-Antoine covered market** is the place to buy vanilla, cinnamon or nutmeg. Here and there, you'll see lovely old buildings among the modern apartment blocks.

On Rue de Nozières, the **Saint-John Perse Museum** in a restored colonial mansion is devoted to the local poet christened Alexis Léger.

In Rue Peynier, the **Schoelcher Museum** recounts the history of the abolition of slavery.

Grande-Terre

Fields of sugar cane cover most of Grande-Terre. The Atlantic crashes against the east coast, while beaches line the southern shore. The stretch from Bas du Fort to Saint-François is Guadeloupe's touristic area.

Bas du Fort

Three formidable cannon greet you at the wooden drawbridge entrance to the coral-stone Fleur d'Epée fort, commanding access to Pointe-à-Pitre's harbour in a residential and touristic district. Late in the 18th century, British and French forces fought bloody battles for this strategic hill. There's a small museum in the fort and, near the marina, an aquarium.

Le Gosier

Contingents of fierce invaders used to put ashore here. Today this is Guadeloupe's riviera, with resort hotels strung along the beaches and tennis courts laid out among the coconut palms.

Sainte-Anne

The island's best beach is near the former sugar capital Sainte-Anne: La Caravelle, owned by Club Med but open to the public.

The coral reefs are clearly visible beneath the limpid water.

Saint-François

This old fishing village has been completely engulfed by hotels and resort facilities: marina, golf course, tennis courts, beaches. You can practise almost every sport imaginable here. Just outside the resort, **Raisins Clairs** is a magnificent beach of golden sand.

La Pointe des Châteaux

One of the scenic highlights of the entire Caribbean, at the eastern tip of the butterfly's wing, is a wildly beautiful cliff formation with rocks shaped like castles lashed and eroded by Atlantic waves. From the summit the view is magnificent: the large island in the distance is La Désirade, the small Petite-Terre islets are much closer.

Le Moule

From Saint-François, the road to Le Moule runs through great fields of sugar cane dotted here and there with reminders of the good old days: ruined sugar mills, grand plantation houses. The **Damoiseau distillery** at Bellevue is open for visits.

The once-flourishing port of Le Moule has a charming beach, **L'Autre Bord**, and the **Edgar-Clerc Archaeological Museum** housing an interesting collection of pre-Columbian artefacts dating from Arawak and Carib times.

The North

On the east coast, **Porte d'Enfer** (Hell's Gate) is a strange fjord-like lagoon whose waters are delightful for bathing. Further north, **Pointe de la Grande Vigie** offers spectacular views; on a clear day you can see La Désirade across 40 km (25 miles) of blue ocean, and even further to Antigua and the peaks of Montserrat.

On the road back to Pointe-à-Pitre, **Souffleur** beach at Port-Louis has gorgeous turquoise waters. Stop off at **Morne-à-l'Eau** to see the strange cemetery with tombs completely covered with black and white chequerboard ceramics.

Mangrove swamps stretch all down the west coast. Almost unreachable except by boat, they are rewarding for fishermen and birdwatchers.

Basse-Terre

Columbus called it the Emerald Isle. Halted by the volcanic mass of La Soufrière, clouds empty over the land, watering banana and coffee plantations and tropical forest. Along the coast, beaches and villages huddle in bays protected from the winds and hemmed by coconut palms.

SUGAR CANE

The origins of the cultivation of sugar cane *(Saccharum officinarum)* are lost in the mists of time. However, it is believed that it was used for the first time in the Ganges basin. The word "sugar", derived from the Sanskrit "sarkara", tends to prove this theory. Brought to the Mediterranean by Arab merchants, sugar was unknown in Europe until after the Crusades, and at first it was called "pagan honey". For several centuries it was a luxury product, reserved for the elite. On his second journey, Christopher Columbus introduced sugar cane to America. Cultivation developed in the English and French islands from the second half of the 17th century, and soon afterwards, rum was invented. In the early days, sugar was exported to Europe in the form of syrup or molasses, then, around the end of the 18th century, as light brown *cassonade* (soft crystals). The final refining process to white crystals is usually carried out in European refineries.

The people of Guadeloupe consider sugar cane cultivation to be their iron and steel industry. From February to June, the cane is harvested by hand, after the fields have been burned to rid them of snakes and dry undergrowth. Each cane is cut as close as possible to the ground, where the sugar content is the most concentrated. The cane is then tied into bundles and taken to the mill where it is shredded then crushed under great rollers to extract the juice. This grey or dark green liquid is then fermented and distilled into rum, or evaporated and crystallized to make sugar. The dry residue is generally used for heating the boilers.

istockphoto.com/Logan

Jardin botanique

At Deshaies, the beautifully landscaped botanical garden was created in 2001 in the grounds of a magnificent residence that belonged to the French comedian and actor Coluche (1944–86).

Parc national de la Guadeloupe

The only inland road, the D23, links the east coast with Mahaut on the west side of the island. It meanders through the Guadeloupe national park, a majestic forest of mahogany, ferns, lianas and orchids. **Cascade aux Ecrevisses** (Crayfish Falls) is a lovely picnic area where you can swim in the rocky, fern-carpeted pool beneath the waterfall. A little further, the **Maison de la Forêt** is the departure point for numerous forest trails.

West Coast

Grey sand and pebbles line the deep blue sea, as the road follows the contours of capes and bays, climbing and falling into flower-filled hamlets. From Malendure Beach, excursions can be arranged to **Pigeon Islet**, an underwater reserve where you can dive or take a trip in a glass-bottomed boat.

From Bouillante southwards, the landscape gets drier as the rains are withheld by the Soufrière volcano.

The little town of **Basse-Terre**, smaller and sleepier than Pointe-à-Pitre, may remind you of a French provincial town except for its tropical seaside setting at the foot of La Soufrière's slopes. Its Fort Saint-Charles dates from 1645.

La Soufrière

Temperamental and magnificent, even if its peak is almost always draped in clouds, La Soufrière is a semi-active volcano. From its height of 1,467 m (4,813 ft), it dominates the lush and rugged south of Basse-Terre. In the summer of 1976, it began erupting with low-grade vapour explosions which provoked the evacuation of 72,000 residents at great cost, but nothing else happened. The volcano again gave angry signs of life in 1999, and is carefully monitored.

Southern Tip

From Trois-Rivières, boats cross over to the islands of Les Saintes in under half an hour. Just below the port, the archaeological park of **Roches Gravées** is a small botanical garden containing over 200 Arawak rock engravings.

After Bananier, an asphalted road leads into the eastern slopes of La Soufrière, passing through several plantations of tropical flowers and past a turnoff to the placid lake of **Grand Etang**, to the **Chutes du Carbet**. Two of these three delightful waterfalls, cascading amid a tangle of ferns and tree vines, can be viewed from a platform. The second fall has been closed to the public for safety reasons but you can walk to the others (count 4 hours for the highest, there and back).

East Coast

Back on the coast road, just before Capesterre, twin rows of majestic royal palms line the **Allée Dumanoir**, named after the man who planted the trees. Further north, you will notice a Hindu temple built by the descendants of Indian immigrants brought in to work the sugar plantations after the abolition of slavery.

Sainte-Marie is the spot where Christopher Columbus landed in 1493, and his bust has pride of place in the village square.

From Petit-Bourg, a short detour takes you to **Valombreuse park**, with its extravagant display of tropical flowers.

Marie-Galante

Large and round, and noted for the rum from its extensive sugar cane fields, Marie-Galante was named by Columbus after the ship that brought him across the Atlantic on his second voyage. The island has a number of fine white-sand beaches, notably **Moustique** and **Anse du Vieux Fort** both north of Saint-Louis, **La Feuillère** and **Petite Anse** near Capes-

terre. East of Grand Bourg, in the middle of a 17th-century plantation, **Château Murat** has an interesting old sugar mill.

The atmosphere is simple and relaxed, the people very kind, the Creole food good. The best rum in the world, they say, is made here: you can visit the distilleries and perhaps see the sugar cane arriving by ox-drawn cart.

La Désirade

Beautiful beaches lure the determined few off the beaten track to the little island of La Désirade, its name signifying yearned-for. This was the first of the Antilles spotted by Columbus in 1493. If you like early nights and lazy days, you'll enjoy La Désirade, home to 1,900 people, who are concentrated mainly on the south coast. A single road, 10 km (6 miles) long, links Grande Anse, in the west, via Le Souffleur to the superb **Baie-Mahaut** in the east. At Baie-Mahaut you can see the ruins of the former lepers' colony.

Les Saintes

The eight islands of Les Saintes form a miniature archipelago just 10 km (6 miles) south of Guadeloupe's Basse-Terre. Only two are inhabited, by descendants of the first Breton and Norman settlers, who still talk with a 17th-century French provincial accent. Because the land was too arid for cultivation, the settlers turned to fishing, and now the Saintois are said to be the best sailors of the Antilles. Their distinctive long keel-less boats, also called *saintois*, are used all around Guadeloupe, while their conical straw hats, or *salako*, have been relegated to the realm of souvenirs.

Bourg des Saintes

The majority of the 2500 inhabitants live on Terre-de-Haut, the smallest but also the loveliest of the islands. Red-roofed houses nestle on the surrounding hills, and by the harbour, women and children welcome the boats with smiles and irresistible coconut tarts, *tourments d'amour*.

On the main square, a monument commemorates the French Revolution and the town hall flies a red, white and blue flag honouring the "mother country".

Fort Napoléon

Built in the 19th century, the fort was restored a few years ago and now houses an interesting museum of local history. It looks out over the north side of Terre-de-Haut and offers fine views of Guadeloupe and Marigot Bay.

Beaches

Safely sheltered behind a rampart of eroded rocks, **Pont-Pierre** (or Pompierre) Bay boasts a magnificent semi-circular sandy strip of beach. On the Atlantic coast, opposite Bourg des Saintes, **Grande Anse** is spectacular, but dangerous for swimming.

To the south, the Pain de Sucre peninsula is rimmed by two stretches of fine sand. **Anse Crawen** is a nudists' beach and offers the best snorkelling and skin diving.

Trafalgar of the Antilles

Christopher Columbus called the islands Los Santos in honour of All Saints Day. Settled in the 17th century by fishermen from Brittany and Normandy, the islands became a stake in the rivalry between France and England. On August 4, 1666, Lord Willoughby invaded the Saintes waters with 2,000 men in 18 warships. The islands were defended by two French ships commanded by Baron and Beauville. A violent hurricane annihilated most of the English fleet, but they were not defeated until Dulion arrived on August 15 with 200 allied Dominican Caribs, who obliged the few survivors to surrender. On April 12, 1782, in the channel of Les Saintes, a fleet led by Admiral Rodney marked a historic victory against France's Admiral de Grasse. This disastrous French naval defeat is known as the Battle of Les Saintes.

Arrival by air into Saint-Barthélemy is something you'll never forget!

Marc Michel

Saint-Barthélemy

This just might be the best piece of France anywhere. Known as "St Barts" or St-Barth in French (Columbus gave his brother's name, Bartolomeo, to the island when he sailed past in 1493), it's peaceful and picturesque, with roller-coaster hills, rocky coves and powdery beaches lining a limpid, emerald sea.

Twittering in the shrubbery of its 25 sq km (10 sq miles) are thousands of birds: yellowbreasts, redthroats and hummingbirds. Many of the 8,500 inhabitants are descendants of Huguenots from Brittany and Normandy. These unusual Frenchmen, and the handful of black families that have also lived here for generations, strike visitors as extremely kind, open and unpretentious.

At many points around St Barts and its small rocky offshore islets, there is fine reef snorkelling. Scuba divers and underwater photographers will never get bored.

Gustavia

You'll soon understand why Gustavia's rectangular harbour is a favourite with the Caribbean yachting set. From this ideal anchorage you can rent small excursion- or fishing boats, or charter a floating palace. Or join the onlooking landlubbers at one of the cafés ringing the harbour. Behind the town's pretty red-roofed houses rises a backdrop of hills. In one morning you can get to know just about everybody in this unassuming island capital. The Swedes declared it a free port in 1785, and its status has not yet changed. Here and there you'll note a Swedish touch: the Swedish flag beside the French on St Barts' coat of arms (as you can see in the town hall); the old Swedish clock tower in green-painted wood; and the shopping streets bearing Swedish names.

Leeward

The seascapes and panoramas on this island are enough to tempt any driver to glance away from the serviceable but narrow roads. Winding and hilly, they are veritable labyrinths, many finishing at signposted dead-ends. From Gustavia, a road leads to the **Col de la Tourmente**, an important crossroads where the main activity is watching the planes skimming over the hilltop before diving into the airport at Saint-Jean Bay. **Anse des Cayes** unfurls its golden carpet of sand below the handsome Hotel Manapany. Another branch takes you to **Flamands**, a pretty village set along a curving beach (the current can be strong here), then on to Petite Anse.

Coconut palms and sloping cliffs ring the tranquil waters of **Colombier**, north of Gustavia. This beach of magnificent tan sand is most easily reached by boat. On foot, you'll have to walk for about 20 minutes down a stony track to this paradise bay which American banker David Rockefeller chose as the site of a holiday home. You can see the hazy outline of Saint-Martin out to sea.

On the south coast, **Corossol** is a fishing village where the grannies wear traditional costume and the fishermen set to sea in boats of many colours.

Kiss-me-not. For Sunday mass, old ladies in St-Barthélemy still wear the white cotton bonnet brought here by their Norman ancestors three centuries ago. Its French name, *quichenotte*, derives from the English kiss-me-not; it probably protected delicate cheeks from the hot sun, though it's said it was invented to stop English soldiers dallying with French women.

hemis.fr/Du Boisberranger

Windward

There's no access problem to **Saint-Jean**, the best known of St Barthélemy's beaches. Swimming in this bay is perfect. The beach is actually two shimmering crescents of pale sand separated by a small rocky promontory and sheltered by a coral reef.

At **Lorient** on the north coast, the island's first settlement, visit the church built with island stone—hauled here by boat and filed down to size by the townswomen. Inside, conch shells do duty as holy water basins.

Not far away is **Pointe Milou**, a wild, breathtaking headland from which, on a clear day, you can count nine isles or rocks in the sea. Strange cactus-like plants with red nobbles growing here in great profusion are called Têtes à l'Anglais (Englishman's heads). They may have been named after the British redcoats.

From the highest point of the road encircling Morne Vitet, on the eastern part of the island, stop to take in the sweeping view over a bay called **Grand Cul-de-Sac**, favoured by windsurfers, and out to Tortue islet in the Atlantic.

The south coast has two pleasant beaches in neighbouring coves: **Grande Saline** and **Gouverneur**. Sea grapes and shrubs provide little shade here; otherwise you should find no fault with either of these strands.

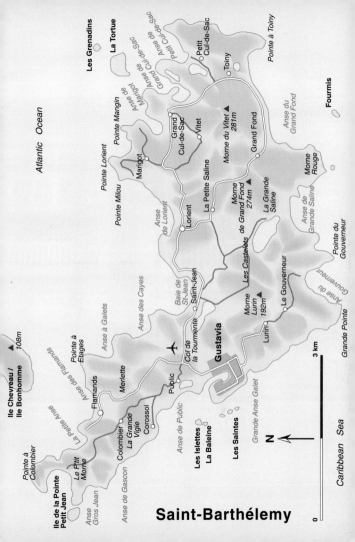

Saint-Barthélemy

Philipsburg: a colourful place to discover at snail's pace.

hemis.fr / Pérousse

Saint-Martin/ Sint Maarten

Two countries, two flags, two power stations (one 110 V and the other 220), two airports and three currencies: the island can qualify as having one of the world's longest governmental love affairs: since 1648 the French and Dutch have shared sovereignty in almost total harmony. Three-fifths of the area belongs to France. Theoretically there is a frontier, but there isn't a single customs official and it has always been unguarded. In any case, the island is free of levies on any imported goods, which still means completely duty-free shopping today.

Dutch Side

A popular stopover for cruise ships, the Dutch capital, Philipsburg is a lively place, its wooden churches, painted houses and Indonesian restaurants vying for space with luxury hotels and casinos. It also has the island's only international airport.

Philipsburg

Cruise ships tie up opposite **Wathey Square**, where the old courthouse dates from 1793. **Front Street**, parallel to the shore, is the main thoroughfare lined with hotels, casinos, restaurants and, of course, duty-free shops. Prices here are up to 50 per cent cheaper than in Europe. At No. 119, a small museum traces the history of the island.

East of the beach, the marinas of **Bobby** and **Great Bay** are the departure point for sailing ships and boats to Saint-Barthélemy.

West of town, **Fort Amsterdam** lies in ruins but affords fabulous views over the bay.

Dual personality. Saint-Martin/Sint Maarten was first settled in the 1630s by France and Holland. In a struggle with Spain over the island's Dutch settlements, Governor Peter Stuyvesant (later Governor of New York) lost a leg. Spain finally gave up its claim, and in 1648 France and the Netherlands signed a treaty agreeing to share sovereignty of Saint-Martin. During the first half of the 18th century the British became interested in France's Caribbean possessions and managed to seize the island briefly three times. The treaty ending the Seven Years' War between Britain and France left French Saint-Martin definitely in Gallic hands. Ownership of the island was eventually shared between the Netherlands and France in 1816. From the 1940s to mid 2007, when it changed status, the French part of the island was a sub-prefecture of Guadeloupe. After 54 years as part of the Netherlands Antilles, Sint-Maarten became an autonomous entity within the Kingdom of the Netherlands.

istockphoto.com/Walsh

A splash of colourful rooftops over-looking Orient Beach on Saint-Martin.

Beaches

Beyond the airport are some of the best of the island's 36 beaches: **Simsonbaai**, the resorts of **Mahobaai** and **Mulletbaai** and, beyond, **Cupecoy Bay**, beneath a little cliff. The water, sapphire blue or emerald green, is irresistible.

French Side

Much of the French side's charm is that it seems content to slumber languidly in the sun. Lingering over a seaside dinner is the preferred after-dark activity.

Marigot

Tourism is beginning to develop in the capital, and the last wooden houses of Rue de la Liberté will soon all be replaced by duty-free shops. Near the quayside, the morning market brings a touch of colour to the port. The fishermen chug home with their catch to a clamorous welcome; nearby, ladies perch on little stools and sell breadfruit and cinnamon. Inter-island cargoes arrive with straw-hatted voyagers, and livestock tethered haphazardly.

The **Musée de Marigot**, in a modern building, is an archaeological museum mainly devoted to the Arawak Indians.

For the view over Marigot Bay, it's worth the four-minute climb up to deserted **Fort Saint-Louis**. This 17th-century bastion certainly looks its age; there isn't much left of it. Sheep graze alongside a rusty cannon.

Grand-Case

A few minutes up and over the hill by car, this village strung unpretentiously along a curving beach is known for its high-quality French restaurants. To the south, the **Pic du Paradis** offers a fine view of the island. At the salt flats nearby is the tiny airport, used for local flights.

Beaches

Orient Beach, a marvellous stretch of white sand lapped by crystal-clear waters is one of the best; the bay is a marine reserve. The southern part is strictly for nudists. Trips from here take you to **Ilet Pinel** and **Caye Vert**, small islets close to shore, or, further out to sea, **Tintamarre Island**. Beautiful Oyster Pond is a resort on a protected bay.

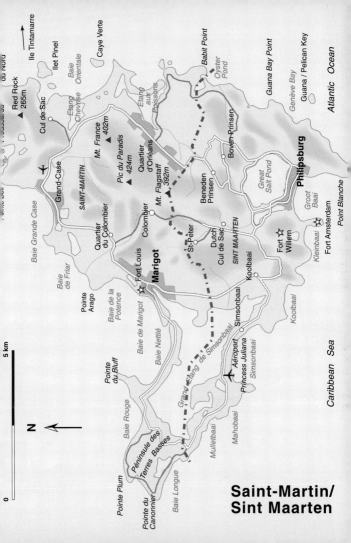

Saint-Martin/
Sint Maarten

A riot of detail on the façade of the Schoelcher Library.

Claude Hervé-Bazin

Martinique

The Indians called it Madinina—island of flowers, and they were right: hibiscus and bougainvillaea, magnolia and oleander, anthurium, poinsettia and more, all compete to make Martinique one of the most colourful tropical gardens on earth.

When Columbus discovered the island, he called it "the best, most fertile, sweetest, most charming country in the world" and named it Matinino, probably after Saint Martin (or, some say, as an approximation of Madinina), a name which the French later adapted to Martinique.

Fort-de-France

Clinging to its superb harbour, Martinique's capital is sometimes bustling, sometimes drowsy—but always captivating. Awesome green mountains form the backdrop while strikingly tall palm trees dwarf all but a very few buildings.

La Savane

Visitors and Martiniquais alike tend to gravitate towards the landscaped park called La Savane near the water's edge in the heart of the city. Pierre Belain d'Esnambuc, the Norman adventurer who first claimed Martinique for France, has a statue here, but cast in bronze. Though you'd never guess it, the French fought bloody battles against the English and Dutch on La Savane. On the north side of the park stands a white marble statue of Napoleon's Josephine, holding a rose. But she has been decapitated—for having encouraged Napoleon to re-introduce slavery in 1802.

Alongside La Savane runs rue de la Liberté, and at No. 9 is Martinique's excellent **Archaeological Museum**. Of particular interest is the collection of Arawak and Carib objects, including engraved cups and remarkable decorative painted figurines.

Town Centre

The teeming shopping area centres on the market on rue Isambert and boulevard Allègre. Here you'll have your pick of fresh Martinique pineapples, coconut slices or the pungent baby limes so loved in the West Indies. Among the bananas and Caribbean sweet potatoes, you'll find bottles of old-time patent medicines for sale. If you are here early enough, cross the "canal" (the Madame River) to get to the fish market; it's fascinating to watch the vendors preparing their wares for sale with machetes.

It's hard to miss **St-Louis Cathedral**, a vast metallic structure. The same architect, Henri Pick, designed the startling **Schoelcher Library** on rue de la Liberté, a strange blend of Byzantine and contemporary styles. This odd but attractive town house was on display at the 1889 Paris World's Fair, then dismantled, shipped to Martinique and re-constructed.

For an unrivalled view of the town, climb up to the **Calvaire chapel** through the Didier residential district with its handsome colonial houses.

West Coast

The coast road leaves Fort-de-France by Schoelcher beach, affording scenic views of the sea and colourful fishing craft pulled up onto the pebbles. **Case-Pilote**, one of the oldest villages of Martinique, has a venerable baroque church built of stone in the centre, and an enchanting main square complete with fountain and old town hall. The large town of **Carbet**, where Columbus and Belain d'Esnambuc disembarked, owes its name to the original settlement founded by Amerindians. Nowadays the Neisson distillery attracts plenty of visitors.

Further north, **Anse Turin** has acquired a certain renown ever since someone remembered that Gauguin came here in 1887. The small museum, facing the beach, documents the painter's five-month stay, before he set off for Tahiti.

The **Vallée des Papillons**, on the ruins of a 17th-century plantation, comprises a botanical garden and butterfly house.

Saint-Pierre

It was a lovely seaside town, the first French settlement on Martinique, the "Paris of the West Indies". When 1,397-m (4,583-ft) Mont Pelée began to belch smoke and cinders far above Saint-Pierre on April 24, 1902, authorities professed no concern. Evacuation was unthinkable—an election was coming up. By May 2, the ash had reached Saint-Pierre. The

Joséphine. Marie-Josèphe Rose Tascher de La Pagerie was born on June 23, 1763, at the Petite Guinée, her parents' plantation. Aged 16, she set sail for France where she married the son of a former governor of the Windward Isles, Viscount de Beauharnais. Two children were born, Eugène and Hortense, but the marriage was not a happy one and finally Marie-Josèphe returned to Martinique.
In 1790, during the Terror, her husband was guillotined. Back in France, in 1796 she remarried a promising army general, six years younger than herself: Napoleon Bonaparte, who called her Joséphine. In 1809, Emperor Napoleon repudiated her, as she had not given him a successor.

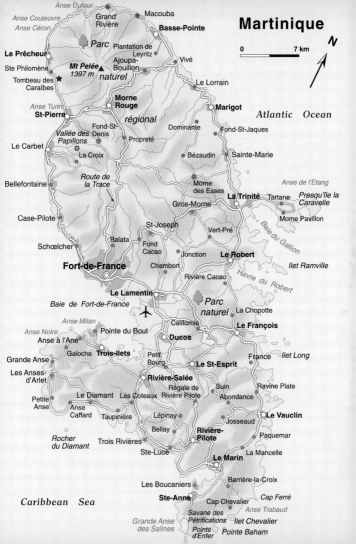

next day, the village of Le Prêcheur was shrouded in darkness. Another two days later, a mass of mud and rocks was swept down by Pelée's White River (Rivière Blanche), destroying the Guérin sugar factory and killing 25 people. At the same time a tidal wave lashed the shores near Saint-Pierre. Flames began spouting from the mountain's peak, and some of the residents began to panic. On May 7 the governor of Martinique arrived with his wife to reassure the population, which numbered around 30,000 at the time. During the night of the 7th and 8th, a huge wave of mud swept over the villages of the north coast. But the authorities remained blind to the danger and persuaded the people to stay calm. In the morning, a soothing notice was posted on the walls of Fort-de-France, but there wasn't time for it to reach Saint-Pierre: the volcano erupted at precisely 7.50 a.m. A burning cloud of gas and steam bearing rocks, lava and ashes roared down the mountainside onto the town. In just three minutes Saint-Pierre was totally wiped out. The only survivor was a certain Cyparis, prisoner in a thick-walled dungeon. For years afterwards he was displayed abroad as an attraction of Barnum circus. Less than three months later, another eruption destroyed the eastern slope of the volcano, killing a thousand.

The eruption is documented in the historical and vulcanological museums, where old photographs show the town as it was before disaster struck, and objects of molten glass, twisted metal and burnt food illustrate the wreckage. You can walk through the ruined town and see the church, fort, theatre and the prison that saved the life of Cyparis. At the north exit of town, the **CDST** is a scientific centre examining the vulcanology of Mont Pelée.

Northern Beaches

Black sand beaches nestle in the folds of the cliffs all round the northern end of the island. The

fotolia.com/Perinelle

Mancenillier. Native to the West Indies, the small mancenillier tree *(Hyppomane mancenilla)* which grows on the beaches, is extremely dangerous. Its white, milky sap contains Prussic acid—a violent poison—in sufficient quantity to burn anyone who comes into contact with it. Even rainwater dripping from the branches can burn holes in clothing. The fruit resemble crab apples but are also toxic.

Tombeau des Caraïbes is where the last Indians of Martinique are said to have jumped to their deaths to escape colonization.

The old village of **Le Prêcheur**, fringed by green and orange rubber trees along the shore, was the childhood home of Françoise d'Aubigné, who later in life became Madame de Maintenon, the wife of Louis XIV.

The road ends at **Anse Céron**, a superb beach shaded by coconut palms. The humble sugar plantation of the same name still has the little houses where slaves are lodged. Offshore, **Ilet la Perle** is a good diving spot. A footpath leads to Anse Couleuvre and beyond into the tropical forest to **Grand'Rivière**, a fishing village.

Route de la Trace

The Jesuits opened this road through the forest in the 17th century. Emerging from the vegetation, **Balata church** is an amazing reduced-size replica of the Sacré-Cœur basilica in Paris. The magnificent **Jardin de Balata**, with a view of the Carbet peaks *(pitons)*, displays over a thousand varieties of tropical plants where hummingbirds come to feed, and you can visit a little Creole house furnished in the traditional way. A waterfall tumbles into the gorge at the **Site de l'Alma**. The road takes you to Morne-Rouge at the foot of Mont Pelée, where you can

Beach of black volcanic sand at **Anse Céron**.

visit the **Macintosh anthurium nursery**. The volcano has shown no sign of erupting since the 1930s but is closely monitored. Learn all about it at the information centre, **La Maison du Volcan**.

Atlantic Coast

In 1976, the French and American presidents met at the **Leyritz Plantation**. The vast domain, created around 1700, is now a hotel. The old mansion is still furnished with the original pieces, and the outbuildings include a mill and sugar refinery. The souvenir shop also has a **Musée de Figurines végétales**, traditional dolls made from banana leaves.

At **Fond-Saint-Jacques**, the Dominican monastery was founded in 1658, and in its time was the most important industrial centre of the island. For it was here, under the guidance of Father Labat, that the "cognac" method of distilling rum was invented.

Looking green, fresh and innocuous, the volcano of Mont Pelé.

hemis.fr/Frances

The site has been restored and gives insight into the Antilles sugar industry.

At Sainte-Marie, the **Rum Museum** of the Saint-James Distillery traces the history of sugar cane and the national drink from 1765 to the present day. Nearby **Morne-des-Esses** is noted for its basketwork crafted in the Carib tradition.

The Caravelle peninsula has two pretty beaches at the northern end, **Tartane** and **Anse l'Etang**. At the tip, in a natural reserve, lie the ruins of the 17th-century **Château Dubuc**. Further south, **Baie du Robert**, dotted with tiny isles, is superb for boat trips over the white sands around the reefs, and the same can be said for **Le François**.

Inland, the **Domaine de l'Acajou** is home to the Habitation Clément, an 18th-century mansion furnished in antiques with a distillery famous for its aged rum.

The South

Trois Ilets, south of Fort-de-France, is the home-town of Marie-Josèphe Rose Tascher de la Pagerie—better known as the famous Joséphine, wife of Napoleon and Empress of France. In her childhood home, now the **Musée de la Pagerie**, you can see a photocopy of her wedding certificate, family portraits, and a passionate love-letter sent by Napoleon from Italy in 1796.

You might also like to look in at the **Maison de la Canne**, a museum devoted to sugar, and the **Musée du Café et du Cacao**.

Continue round the coast past Pointe du Bout, with its marina and resort hotels, the grey-sand beach of Anse à l'Ane, and the pretty village Les Anses d'Arlet, and you'll suddenly be confronted by a gigantic and ominous-looking bulk rising straight up out of the sea. **Diamond Rock** (Rocher du Diamant) was occupied by the Royal Navy as a strategic base during the struggle for Martinique in 1804. Elevated to the rank of a ship, *H.M.S. Diamond Rock* bombarded French positions and ships for 17 months until the French finally tricked the British by arranging for a boat full of rum to run aground there one night.

You can take a guided tour of the **Trois Rivières Distillery**, which produces half of the island's rum.

From Sainte-Luce onwards, hotels stand in line along the best beaches. **Le Marin**, at the end of a deep bay, has a large marina and a church dating from 1766. One beautiful beach succeeds another as far as **Sainte-Anne**, a village rapidly being transformed into a resort. Its best-known beach is **Les Salines**, ten minutes to the east: a vast stretch of fine sand lapped by warm water and shaded by coconut palms.

THE HARD FACTS

Airports. Pôle Caraïbes (PTP), 3 km (2 miles) from Point-à-Pitre; Martinique Aimé Césaire (FDF), at Le Lamentin, 11 km (7 miles) from Fort-de-France; Princess Juliana (SXM), 15 km (9 miles) west of Philipsburg. Inter-island flights serve Grand-Case airport on Saint-Martin, and there are several flights daily between Guadeloupe and St-Barth, Les Saintes, Marie-Galante and La Désirade.

Banks. Open Monday to Friday, with hours varying from one island to another. Some open Saturday morning. On days preceding public holidays, they close at noon.

Climate. Winter is the dry season; summer is hotter and wetter. Rainfall is heavier from mid-June to mid-August and October to November, and there are risks of hurricanes from July to September. The climatic conditions vary from one side of each island to the other. On the coast, average temperatures range from 25°C to 30°C, day and night, relieved by tradewinds from the Atlantic.

Clothing. Take lightweight clothes and a warm sweater for cool evenings and trips into the mountains. Do not wander around town in beachwear.

Communications. Country codes: Guadeloupe, dependencies, Saint-Barthélemy and Saint-Martin 590, Sint-Maarten 599, Martinique 596. International dialling code from all islands: 00. Internet access is provided in major hotels, and you will find Internet cafés in the main towns.

Customs Allowance. Visitors coming to Guadeloupe or Martinique from non-EU countries and 17 years or older may import, duty-free, 200 cigarettes or 50 cigars or 250 g tobacco, 1 litre of spirits over 22° or 2 litres up to 22°, 2 litres of wine, 50 g perfume and 250 ml eau de toilette. Saint-Martin/Sint-Maarten is a duty-free zone and no tax is payable on any items imported or exported. However, you may have to pay duty on items purchased on the island when you return home.

Driving. Hiring a car is the ideal way to visit the islands. Prices are competitive, but ask if insurance is included. You need a national driving licence and at least one year's driving experience. Guadeloupe's roads are modern and well-maintained, but those on the other islands tend to be winding, hilly and in places bumpy. Its best to avoid driving after nightfall as there are many invisible dangers such as cyclists, animals and unlit tractors. Driving is on the right. Speed limits are 120 kph on motorways, 50 kph in built-up areas and 90 kph on other roads, except in Saint-Barthélemy where the limit on all roads is 45 kph.

Electricity. 220 volts 50/60 Hz everywhere except the Dutch Sint-Maarten where it is 110 volts, 60 Hz.

Holidays. January 1, New Year's Day; January 6, Epiphany (St Martin); May 1, Labour Day; May 8, Victory Day; May 22 Abolition of Slavery (Martinique), May 27, Abolition of Slavery (Guadeloupe, St-Barthélemy); July 14, Bastille Day; July 21, Victor Schoelcher Day; August 15, Assumption; November 1, All Saints' Day; November 11, Armistice Day; December 25, Christmas. Moveable: February-March, Lenten Carnival; Ash Wednesday (except St-Martin); March-April, Good Friday (St-Martin), Easter Monday; May–June, Ascension Day; Whit Monday.

   Sint-Maarten: New Year; Easter, Labour Day, Ascension Day, Christmas, and April 30, Queen's Birthday; October 21, Antilles Day; November 11, Sint Maarten Day, December 25 and 26 Christmas.

Language. The official language is French, but Creole is also widely spoken. English is understood in touristic areas, and practically supersedes French in Saint-Martin/Sint Maarten.

Money. On Guadeloupe, Martinique and Saint-Martin, the Euro is used, as in Metropolitan France. Coins from 1 centime to 2 euros; banknotes from 5 to 500 euros. The main credit cards and travellers cheques (preferably in euros) are accepted. On Sint-Maarten, the Netherlands Antilles guilder or florin (NAf or ANG) divided into 100 cents. Coins range from 1 cent to 5 NAf, banknotes from 10 to 100 NAf. Credit cards and travellers cheques (preferably in euros or US dollars) are widely accepted. On this island and St-Barthélemy, prices are also given in US dollars.

Time. GMT–4, all year round.

Tipping. It is usual to leave a tip equivalent to 10% of the bill.

Transport. The easiest way to get around the islands is to hire a car, but there are also plenty of local buses and collective taxis.

Water. Bottled mineral water is widely available and is advised.

A phone link to home directly from the beach.

istockphoto.com/McFrame

WEST INDIES

This section describes the English-speaking islands of the long green garland sweeping down to the coast of Venezuela, also called the Lesser Antilles, or the Leeward and Windward Isles. From Anguilla to Trinidad and Tobago, these lush fragments of paradise are perfect for getting away from it all.

Anguilla

Imagine a long, slender coral island lying lazily in the eastern Caribbean, with more than thirty superlative beaches fringing its shores. Then visualize the vibrant marine life in its coral reefs waiting to be explored. That's Anguilla. Best of all, you can still have some of those beaches virtually to yourself, despite the increasing numbers of visitors discovering this sleepy isle.

The population of 15,500 is descended mostly from Africans, although more and more North Americans and Europeans are joining them for an interesting cultural mosaic. Traditionally the islanders have lived from salt production, lobster fishing, agriculture and livestock-raising. Tourism is now the major source of revenue.

Boat races are frequently held. The craft are a special wooden sloop made locally. The most noteworthy races, enlivened by non-stop parties, take place during Carnival Week in August.

The low-lying coral island is covered with scrub vegetation. It's a friendly, quiet place, and one of the safest in the Caribbean. While there's no lack of nightlife, you may well prefer to go to bed early and get up with the dawn to swim with the iridescent fish of the reef or sunbathe on the white sands. With a bit of luck, yours may well be the only footprints.

The Valley

The capital, set in the centre of the island, has a population of 1800. The old customs house has been converted into the **National Museum**, where you can discover more about the island's history, flora and fauna. But most visitors never stir from the beachy fringes of the island to investigate The Valley.

ANGUILLA FLASHBACK

Pre-Columbian era
The island is inhabited by Arawaks, until a cannibal tribe, the Caribs, arrive. In 1493 Columbus sights the island and names it Anguilla ("eel"), probably because of its long, thin shape.

17th century
The British colonize the island in 1650. Many of the settlers are Irish from St Kitts. The Amerindians are wiped out by enslavement and disease.

18th century
The population numbers over 1,000, two-thirds of whom are African slaves. The French attack in 1745 and 1796, but are repelled by the islanders.

19th century
Anguilla is incorporated into the colony of St Kitts and Nevis.

20th century–present
In 1967 Anguilla makes a unilateral declaration of independence and expels the St Kitts police force. As negotiations break down between the islanders and the Crown, British paratroopers "invade" the island in 1969 and install a Commissioner. The London Metropolitan Police remain an unusual presence on the island until 1972. Anguilla becomes a British Dependent Territory in 1980, with a Governor to represent the Crown. Tourism becomes important.

istockphoto.com/Geer

St Gerard's Church in The Valley.

Beaches

Whichever one you decide on, you can arrange for a taxi to take you there and pick you up later. Here are the best, running anti-clockwise from Shoal Bay (East), on the northeast coast.

Shoal Bay (East)

This is the most popular beach, and it has more facilities than the others, including beach chairs and umbrellas for rent, snorkels, masks and paddle boats. Snorkelling is easy as pie here, with the closest reef only a stone's throw offshore. A glass-bottom boat makes trips over the reef, and you can hire a fishing boat.

The Fountain, discovered near Shoal Bay, is a cavern containing several freshwater pools, a spring and some petroglyphs. Archaeologists believe this dome-shaped cavern was a major Arawak centre for worship.

At the nearby fishing village, **Island Harbour**, you'll see the lobster catch come in, the fishermen mending their nets and locals hard at work building schooners. You can get transport to many of the cays and islands. **Scilly Cay**, out in the harbour, is one of these: you just have to wave from the shore and a boat will come out to collect you.

Little Bay

Protected by high cliff walls extending into the sea, this is a hideaway beach where you may see

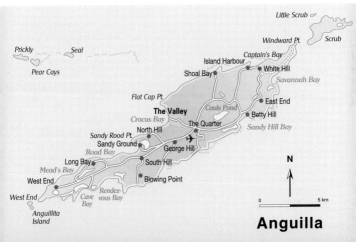

shoals of tiny silver fish shimmering in the blue water. Swim around the cliff wall to the north and you will reach Limestone Bay, a tiny stretch of sand on the Atlantic coast.

Crocus Bay

At the bottom of a steep hill, Crocus Bay offers excellent snorkelling, views of cliffs and fantastic sunsets. You may see fishermen hauling in their trawl nets.

Sandy Ground/Road Bay

Sandy Ground sees a lot of action as the principal port on the island; it has a lively nightlife and plenty of restaurants. Ferries leave every hour for **Sandy Island**, just 20 minutes offshore, where the snorkelling is excellent. Further out are **Prickly Pear Cays** with a sweeping arc of sand, a large population of birds and pelicans, and superb coral gardens. Road Bay beach is quiet and ideal for swimming.

Mead's Bay

The beach has sands like talcum powder a mile long, and some fine restaurants. **Malliouhana Resort** is at the eastern end, **Frangipani** and **Carimar Beach Club** to the west.

Cove Bay

With dunes and coconut palms and just one restaurant, this is a secluded beach; its reef is popular with snorkellers.

Rendezvous Bay

A perfect arc of sand, lined with dunes, the bay has three large resort hotels, all with restaurants. Pretty shells wash up onto the beach.

Blowing Point

A sea port with links to Saint-Martin, Blowing Point has small beaches on both sides. To the east is a small cove with a salt pond which is the perfect spot for bird-watching.

Little Harbour

Hemmed in by low cliffs on the landward side and a reef offshore, the beach is secluded, with shallow water. At **Cinnamon Reef** resort, on the west side, you can rent sports equipment and sailboats.

Sandy Hill Bay

A tiny, protected bay with a sloping, sandy beach that's perfect for children. Local people come here for their family picnics. The snorkelling area offshore has small coral formations and green underwater meadows.

Windward Point Bay

Wild and windswept, at the island's northeast point, this beach is reached by bumpy road, or a hike from Junk's Hole. Carry on to **Captain's Bay** on the north shore, where the surf crashes against the rocks.

Antigua and Barbuda

The outline is what gives Antigua its special attraction—scores of bays and inlets, set with so many beaches that you can stay there a year and never visit the same beach twice. There are 365 of them and they are reckoned to be among the finest in the world. This is not the place for those who want things done by yesterday. The pace of life is easy—Antigua and Barbuda's 71,000 people take their time. That is why cricket is popular—more than a national sport, it's almost a religion.

Corbis/Krist

The game of *warri* is popular in Antigua; the name means "house" and refers to the hollows carved into the wooden board.

St John's

If you are lucky enough to arrive here early on a Friday or Saturday, you will see it come alive at the **Public Market**. This is the focal point of the city life, where housewives bargain noisily with farmers over fruit and vegetables, while fishing boats land their catch at the pier.

Cathedral

St John's Cathedral is one of the most impressive Anglican churches in the Caribbean. Originally constructed in 1683, it has been rebuilt twice. After the 1843 earthquake destroyed the previous cathedral, a structure designed to be quake- and hurricane-proof was devised of pitch pine encased in stone. It has since withstood all tests. The figures of St John the Baptist and St John the Divine at the South Gate are believed to have been captured from one of Napoleon's ships.

National Museum

The 18th-century Court House, the former seat of justice and parliament, now houses the National Museum of Antigua and Barbuda. It contains some fascinating displays on the history of the islands and interesting sporting memorabilia.

Fort James

To the northwest, overlooking the harbour, are the ruins of the fort (1703) which once guarded St John's in pirate days. Vestiges of the ramparts still stand and its cannons point out to sea.

English Harbour

One of the most interesting historical sites of the Caribbean is

ANTIGUA AND BARBUDA FLASHBACK

15th–16th centuries
Columbus sights the island, inhabited by Arawak Indians, on his second voyage in 1493 and names it after the church of Santa María la Antigua in Seville.

17th century
English planters from St Kitts colonize Antigua in 1632. The island is coveted by the French and Spanish, but apart from a brief and bloodless French occupation in 1666, it remains British until independence. Antigua becomes the seat of government of the "Leeward Caribbee Islands". In 1680 the British lease Barbuda to the English Codrington brothers, Christopher and John, who established the island's first sugar plantation 11 years earlier. However, the plantation system is not compatible with Barbuda's infertile soil and poor rainfall. The Codringtons use Barbuda instead to grow supplies and raise animals for their Antigua sugar estates. They also breed slaves, who are known for their physical fitness and tall stature.

18th century
American independence robs Antigua and other islands of their markets, and the plantation economy declines. English Harbour becomes the main British naval base in the Caribbean. Rodney sets out from here to defeat the French fleet in 1782 and to regain Britain's West Indies possessions. Nelson is stationed here in the 1780s as commander-in-chief of the Leeward Islands squadron.

19th century
After the Napoleonic Wars the island's strategic importance declines. An earthquake in 1843 hastens the ruin of the sugar plantations. In 1860 Barbuda is made a dependency of Antigua, which becomes part of a federated Leeward Islands Colony in 1871 and retains the seat of government.

20th century–present
Antigua and Barbuda becomes one of the West Indies Associated States of Britain in 1967 with a new constitution and self-government. Agriculture is revived. Independence is attained in 1981.

Nelson's Dockyard at English Harbour. It was developed in the mid-18th century to shelter British warships protecting the West Indies possessions. It saw its heyday during the War of American Independence and the wars against the French. Admiral Horatio Nelson made it his base in the 1780s, but when ships became too big to negotiate the near-landlocked harbour, the dockyard went into decline and was abandoned in 1889. With growing awareness of the island's tourist potential, it was restored during the 1950s, and now looks much as it did in Nelson's time. The best-restored building is the Admiral's House, furnished in period style and used as a nautical museum. Other restored buildings cater for English Harbour's modern role as a yachting centre.

Clarence House

During his tour of duty, Nelson made friends with one of his cap-

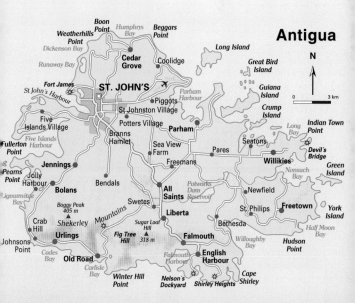

Famous for his zeal, Horatio Nelson was
captain of a frigate ship by the age of 20.

hemis.fr / Barbier

tains, Prince William Henry, Duke of Clarence, who became William IV of England, the Sailor King. Clarence House, built by English masons for the duke, stands on a small hill commanding a fine view of the dockyard.

Dow's Hill Interpretation Centre

A short sound-and-light show illustrates six eras of Antigua's history. The centre also offers fine views over English and Falmouth harbours.

Fig Tree Drive

The scenic route back to St John's takes you through banana groves, forests and hills. The road continues past picturesque west-coast fishing villages and the island's highest point, 405-m (1,330-ft) Boggy Peak.

Barbuda

From St John's airport, it's a mere 15-minute flight to Antigua's sister island, the quintessential unspoilt island paradise. Barbuda is 160 sq km (62 sq miles) of low scrub fringed by a magnificent beach around a lagoon. It counts around 1,500 inhabitants, descendants of slaves, most of them living in the island's only village of **Codrington**. Barbuda's association with Antigua goes back to the 17th century, to the days when it was the private fief of the English Codrington family who used it to raise provisions for their sugar plantations on Antigua and to run a sordid slave-breeding colony.

Barbudans look upon their land as communally owned, and local custom dictates that property can only be leased and not sold to non-Barbudans, and then only by unanimous consent of all the inhabitants. This has served to discourage foreign developers, and today the island is essentially devoid of any major resort infrastructure. Visitors to the handful of hotels like it that way. They come to enjoy the pink-sand beaches, to go deep-sea fishing, snorkelling and scuba-diving round the reefs where there are more than 70 wrecks to explore.

Redonda

Antigua and Barbuda's other dependency is an uninhabited rocky isle which has its own king. The kingdom was founded in 1865 by Matthew Dowdy Shiell, an Irish trader, when he sailed past the island. In 1880 he abdicated in favour of his son Matthew Phipps Shiell, King Felipe I. The title passed to John Gawsworth, a British poet who, as Juan I, created a number of dukes and duchesses from among his literary friends. It is now disputed between King Leo V—historian William Leonard Gates—and novelist Jon M. Wynne-Tyson, plus half a dozen others.

Claude Hervé-Bazin

Huber/Gräfenhain

St Kitts and Nevis

Luscious vegetation in all its tropical brilliance, coconut palms stretching along white or black sand beaches and mysterious, mist-shrouded volcanic mountain peaks make St Kitts and Nevis one of the most desirable resort areas in the Caribbean. The islands remain largely unspoiled, thanks to a sensible policy of controlled development.

Basseterre
The lively little capital has a population of around 13,000. The bustling port area hums with activity as boats of every description come and go. Only two ships at a time can enter the cruise ship dock; the others are served by tenders. A colourful market is held in Basseterre, a mosaic of exotic sights, sounds and smells.

The Circus
With its ornate Victorian clocktower, this square is the heart of Basseterre. The neighbourhood, especially around Fort Street and Independence Square, abounds in shops, cafés and colonial buildings, many of which house administrative offices. As you wander up the side streets, you'll

The mountains of St Kitts often wear a cloak of mist. | Basseterre's Circus and its eye-catching clocktower.

come across tiny shops offering original, hand-made jewellery—simple but decorative pieces made of shell or bone.

Around St Kitts

Most visitors soon head out of Basseterre for a round-the-island tour. Going clockwise, the road leads into vast stretches of sugar cane and cotton plantations.

Old Road Town

It was at the bay just outside town that Sir Thomas Warner, "a man of extraordinary agility of body and good witt" according to an ancient chronicler, landed in 1623. Whatever the motives—some say he had failed to find fresh water on Barbados, others that he planned to start a tobacco plantation on St Kitts that he knew was neglected by the Spaniards—he stayed on, starting a settlement at Sandy Point further up the coast. He also died on St Kitts and was buried in the churchyard of St Thomas, Middle Island. His tomb is inscribed "General of y Caribee".

Wingfield Estate

The manor house was destroyed by fire in 1995 but you can visit the gardens, and their venerable saman tree, more than 350 years old. A batik company has workshops in the grounds, and you can watch the artists creating colourful fabrics. Nearby are some large stones with drawings carved by the island's early Amerindian civilization.

Brimstone Hill Fort

The massive construction, said to have taken 100 years to build—mainly from local volcanic stone—must surely be one of the wonders of the Caribbean world. It was from these majestic battlements, 213 m (700 ft) up, that the British picked off the French galleons with pinpoint accuracy during the many 17th- and 18th-century battles for the island. But the British were not always invincible. In the Battle of Brimstone Hill in 1782, the French won a gallant victory and, for a while, the French flag flew from the warped and battle-scarred fortifications. Today gulls wheel lazily round the ramparts, which command a spectacular view over the Caribbean.

The DL Matheson Visitor Centre presents a video introducing the fort, and there's an interesting museum in the barrack rooms.

Dieppe Bay Town

This resort is of interest mainly to visitors in search of peace and quiet. Good hotels and a pleasant beach make it popular for a relaxing swim and a snack before heading back through the cane fields to Basseterre.

ST KITTS AND NEVIS FLASHBACK

15th–17th centuries
Columbus discovers St Kitts (and sights Nevis) in 1493; he names it St Christopher after himself (and his patron saint). Sir Thomas Warner lands there with his wife, son and a party of thirteen on January 28, 1623, and changes the name to the cosier St Kitts. A hurricane destroys the first tobacco crop in September of the same year. Sir Thomas and Pierre Belain d'Esnambuc of France conclude a treaty (1627) for division of the island, as well as a mutual defence pact against the Spaniards and Carib Indians. Warner starts a settlement on Nevis in 1628. Belain d'Esnambuc attacks the English in 1629 and regular skirmishes between the two occur over the course of the next seven years. Sir Thomas Warner dies in 1648. In 1680 Jamestown (Nevis) is destroyed by earthquake.

18th century
Britain gains St Kitts under terms of the Treaty of Utrecht (1713); the French attack and capture Brimstone Hill Fort in 1782, but return it to the British the following year, as stipulated by the Treaty of Versailles.

19th century
Slaves are emancipated in 1834, but no equitable redistribution of land takes place. The islands of St Kitts, Nevis and Anguilla are united in 1882.

20th century–present
St Kitts-Nevis-Anguilla is established as an independent state in association with Great Britain in 1967. The same year Anguilla seeks independence from St Kitts and is restored to colonial status in 1971. St Kitts and Nevis gain full independence in 1983. The economy flourishes with the development of tourism and with the export of sugar, molasses, Sea Island cotton, coconuts and citrus fruit.

Claude Hervé-Bazin

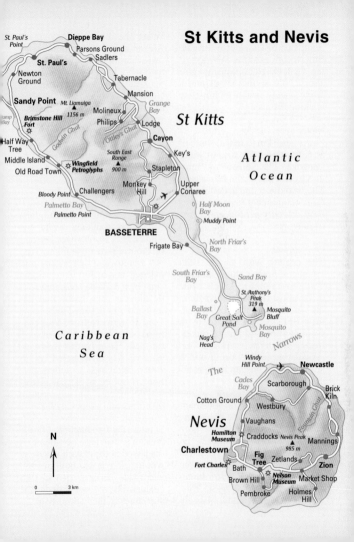

Frigate Bay

Southeast of Basseterre, Frigate Bay Resort, near the fairways of the 18-hole championship golf course, has stylish shops and a white, sandy beach within easy walking distance.

Nevis

Nevis lies 3 km (2 miles) south of St Kitts, across the strip of water known as The Narrows, 45 minutes by fast ferry from Basseterre. The island has fine accommodation, magnificent beaches, good food, friendly people, and an intriguing past.

Charlestown

The capital, with its old Bath Hotel and Spring House (undergoing restoration), was once one of the most fashionable spots in the world. Beribboned 19th-century belles bathed together with their menfolk — assorted dukes, lords, planters, investors and speculators in the spring which still supplies constant hot water.

Museum of Nevis History

Destined to become one of America's most outstanding statesmen, Alexander Hamilton was born in Charlestown on January 11, 1757, the son of Rachel Lavien of Nevis and a Scottish adventurer, James Hamilton. In 1765 James abandoned his family in St Croix, leaving Rachel to fend for herself.

When she died in 1768, young Alexander was left entirely on his own. Through perseverance and hard work he went on to become Secretary of the Treasury in George Washington's cabinet, and helped to draft the US Constitution. He died after a duel on July 11, 1804. A museum is set in the house where he was born and lived for five years. Set in a garden overlooking the sea, it was was restored in 1983.

Horatio Nelson Museum

In 1787, a young sea captain, in a whirlwind romance while his ship *H.M.S. Boreas* was berthed offshore, courted one Fanny Nisbet, a pretty and rich widow, and married her in Fig Tree village church on a Sunday morning. Little did she then know that her husband was destined to become Lord Horatio Nelson, Vice-Admiral of the Fleet. A building near the Bath Hotel houses memorabilia of Nelson donated by an American; it includes letters, pictures, furniture, books and historical documents, and a collection of 17th-century pipes.

St John's Fig Tree Anglican Church

Nelson's marriage certificate is displayed at the church where he was married. It was built in 1680 and twice restored in the 19th century. The register contains the signatures of the happy couple.

MONTSERRAT

A mere dot in the northern Leeward chain, Montserrat is just 11 km (7 miles) long and 18 km (11 miles) across at its widest point. Settled by Spaniards and British, and from 1632 by Irish Catholics fleeing religious oppression on St Kitts, the island became a plantation colony with sugar as the main crop. After the abolition of slavery in 1834, sugar was replaced by limes and, eventually, other orchard and market garden crops. Together with Antigua, St Kitts and Nevis and Anguilla, Montserrat was incorporated in the Territory of the Leeward Islands in 1956 and joined the Federation of the West Indies two years later. Independence was offered in 1966, but the island chose to remain a British Crown Colony. It prided itself on being one of the few unspoiled venues in the eastern Caribbean, until disaster struck in the 1990s. First, Hurricane Hugo caused widespread damage, then in 1995, the Soufrière volcano began to erupt, reaching a climax in 1997, when it covered the island in a blanket of mud and ash. More than half the population fled to Britain and elsewhere, and Plymouth, the capital, was destroyed. To date the volcano is still active. Brades, on the northwest coast, is the provisional capital. In July 2005, Gerald's Airport opened, replacing W.H.Bramble airport destroyed in 1997.

istockphoto.com/Hannah

Dominica

Dominicans call their island the land of the three R's: rivers, rainbows and romance. And that's no exaggeration. Some 365 rivers, one for every day of the year, tumble and cascade through the forest, and rainbows dance over the waterfalls. As for romance, Dominica (pronounced *dominEEca*) can certainly lay claim to being the most ruggedly beautiful of the Caribbean islands, with a mystique that hangs in the air like the perennial fine mist that the islanders term "liquid sunshine".

At the northern end of the Windward chain, the island measures 46 km (29 miles) in length and 25 km (16 miles) wide at the broadest part. A mountainous chain runs from north to south, rising to Morne Diablotin (Devil Mountain) at 1,447 m (4,747 ft).

Roseau

The capital and main port lies in the delta of the Roseau River on the southwest coast. Many of the old colonial buildings have been restored to their former Caribbean charm. But most of the town is a jumble of one or two storey structures with balconies overhanging the pavements. Along the river banks, you'll see a profusion of reeds which gave the town its name. The Caribs used them to make poison-tipped arrows, and they are now essential to the basket-making industry.

Bay Front runs along the harbour; at the northern end, at the mouth of the river, is the **morning market**, particularly animated on Fridays and Saturdays. The original market, where slaves were auctioned and executions carried out, stood near the waterfront and has now been revamped to become the pedestrian zone of Dawbiney Market Plaza.

The **Old Post Office** now houses the tourist office. It is one of the oldest buildings in Roseau, as is Government House, dating back to the 1840s. The **Cathedral of Our Lady of Fair Haven** (1854) boasts carved wooden benches more than 100 years old. One of the stained-glass windows in the side walls depicts Columbus's voyage to the Americas.

Morne Bruce

Behind the town rises the peak of Morne Bruce, the summit affording a good view back over Roseau and the harbour. You can reach it by car along a twisting road or climb the footpath from the **Botanical Gardens** on the southern edge of town. The gardens provide a splendid introduction to the island's flora—orchids, begonias, tiger lilies, flame trees—all of which you will later see on your trips into the mountains and forest. Look out for the intriguing

No-Name tree, unidentified to date. There's also an aviary where the endangered Sisserou and Jaco parrots are bred.

La Vie Domnik Museum
North of Roseau, within walking distance of Canefield Airport, the museum is housed in a former sugar plantation, now the Old Mill Cultural Center. It is well worth visiting to gain invaluable insight into the island's history, geography and culture.

Interior
Any point on the island is only a comfortable day trip away, and there are some fascinating hikes into the mountainous interior to explore the primordial rainforest.

Trafalgar Falls
Situated 8 km (5 miles) northeast of the capital, Trafalgar Falls can be reached by car to the village of Trafalgar and then a 15-minute walk. In a setting of dripping greenery, hot and cold cascades crash and splash into a rocky pool sprouting ferns and orchids. An observation platform gives optimal viewing. The nearby **Papillote Wildlife Retreat** is a nature sanctuary and a paradise for birdwatchers: crested hummingbirds, blue herons and yellow warblers are just three of the 150 colourful species of bird flitting around the ferns and orchids of the garden.

hemis.fr/Gardel

The traditional houses in Roseau have cheerfully painted façades and louvred blinds at the windows.

Sulphur Springs, near the falls, are bubbling pools of grey mud belching sulphurous fumes. The smell of rotten eggs can be picked up over a mile away!

On the way back to Roseau stop at the **d'Auchamps Gardens**, a family estate laid out with wild and cultivated plants, a citrus orchard and traditional Caribbean garden.

Morne Trois Pitons Nat. Park
You can reach the park via three distinct routes. The Laudat Vil-

DOMINICA FLASHBACK

Pre-Columbian era
Carib Indians migrate to the Antilles from the South American mainland and settle on Dominica, ousting the peaceful Arawaks. On Sunday, November 3, 1493, Christopher Columbus sights the island and names it Dominica.

17th–18th centuries
British and French try to settle here in the 17th century, fiercely resisted by the Caribs. With the 1748 Treaty of Aix-la-Chapelle, Britain and France agree to leave Dominica as neutral territory, in the possession of the Caribs. Nonetheless, the fertile soil attracts both French and British planters who attempt to establish themselves. The Peace of Paris in 1763 formally gives Dominica to the British, but the island continues to be juggled between the colonial powers.

19th century–present
In 1805 the French burn down the capital, Roseau, and relinquish their hold on the island only upon payment of £8,000. Between 1833 and 1940, Dominica is governed by the British as part of the Leeward Islands, then it is transferred to the Windward Islands as a separate colony.

In November, 1978, Dominica gains full independence within the Commonwealth. Hurricanes in 1979 and 1980 leave despair and destruction, with 60,000 homeless and the largely agricultural economy in disarray. But Dominica rebuilds, developing its tourist trade with a special emphasis on its unique attractions. Today the population numbers 70,000 (in great majority the descendants of slaves).

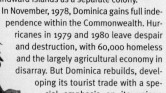

Corbis/Huey

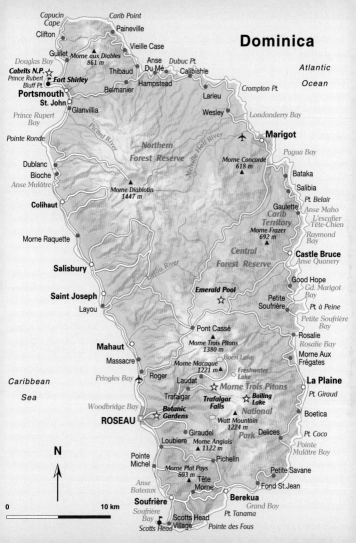

Dominica

Capucin Cape
Carib Point
Paineville
Clifton
Vieille Case
Guillet
Morne aux Diables
861 m
Anse
Du Mé
Dubuc Pt.
Douglas Bay
Calibishie
Thibaud
Cabrits N.P.
Prince Rubert
Bluff Pt.
Fort Shirley
Hampstead
Portsmouth
St. John
Belmanier
Larieu
Crompton Pt.
Glanvillia
Prince Rupert
Bay
Wesley
Londonderry Bay
Pointe Ronde
Northern
Forest Reserve
Marigot
Pagua Bay
Dublanc
Morne Concorde
618 m
Bataka
Bioche
Salibia
Anse Mulâtre
Morne Diablotin
1447 m
Gaulette
Pt. Belair
Anse Maho
Colihaut
Carib
Territory
L'escalier
Tête-Chien
Morne Frazer
692 m
Raymond
Bay
Morne Raquette
Central
Forest Reserve
Castle Bruce
Anse Quanery
Salisbury
Good Hope
Gd. Marigot
Bay
Saint Joseph
Emerald Pool
Petite
Soufrière
Pt. à Peine
Layou
Petite Soufrière
Bay
Pont Cassé
Rosalie
Rosalie Bay
Mahaut
Morne Trois Pitons
1380 m
Morne Aux
Frégates
Massacre
Boeri Lake
Morne Macaque
1221 m
Freshwater
Lake
La Plaine
Pringles Bay
Roger
Laudat
Morne Trois Pitons
Pt. Giraud
Caribbean
Sea
Trafalgar
Trafalgar
Falls
Boiling
Lake
National
Boetica
Woodbridge Bay
Watt Mountain
1224 m
ROSEAU
Botanic
Gardens
Delices
Pt. Coco
Giraudel
Park
Pointe
Mulâtre Bay
Loubiere
Morne Anglais
1122 m
Pichelin
Pointe
Michel
Morne Plat Pays
803 m
Tête
Morne
Petite Savane
Anse
Bateaux
Fond St.Jean
Soufrière
Berekua
Soufrière
Bay
Grand Bay
Pt. Tanama
Scotts Head
Village
Pointe des Fous
Scotts Head

Atlantic
Ocean

N

0   10 km

lage road takes you to the departure point of several marked nature trails, the most popular of which lead to Freshwater Reservoir, Boeri Lake and Boiling Lake. In the lush, dense undergrowth, the plants and trees are labelled for easy identification. The trek to **Freshwater Reservoir** is uphill: it lies at 1,100 m (3,500 ft), its surface dappled with purple water hyacinths. From a grassy knoll, you have a magnificent view of the Atlantic on one side and the Caribbean on the other. The Boeri Lake trail starts at the shores of the reservoir. At an altitude of 853 m (2,800 ft), the lake is almost circular in shape, with a rocky shoreline.

More challenging is the rough 9-km (6-mile) track to the **Valley of Desolation**, taking three or four hours to walk one way. The area lives up to its name with a stark landscape stripped of its vegetation by volcanic upheavals, the last major one in 1880. The eruption also created the **Boiling Lake**, which geologists believe is a flooded crack in the earth (fumarole) rather than a volcanic crater. Escaping gases from the molten lava beneath the lake bring the water temperature to between 180 and 197 °F (82 and 92°C) at the edge and to boiling point in the middle. A cloud of steamy vapour hangs suspended over the lake.

The Cochrane Village road gives access to the **Middleham Falls**, which shoot down into a funnel emptying into a clear, round pool. On the way to the falls you pass the aptly named **Stinking Hole**, a deep crevice in the ground that thousands of bats have chosen for home.

From the Pont Cassé to Castle Bruce road, an easy trail leads to the ethereal **Emerald Pool**, a delightful grotto fed by a clear waterfall plunging over the edge of a fern-clad cliff. This northern section of the national park is also the start of climbs to the summit of Morne Trois Pitons, rising to some 1,400 m (4,600 ft).

Layou River Valley

North of Roseau, the valley has been densely cultivated with an almost unbelievable variety and profusion of crops. Look out for plantations of grapefruit, banana, passionfruit, limes, tobacco and cocoa. The river is Dominica's longest; tubing excursions are organized.

West Coast

The road runs north from Roseau to the island's second town, Portsmouth. The scenic drive is both exhilarating and heart-stopping, punctuated by hairpin bends, steep gradients and tunnels, with spectacular views round every turn.

Portsmouth

Gaily painted wooden houses with flower-filled gardens line the streets that run parallel to Prince Rupert Bay. South of town you can take a trip along **Indian River**, gliding in a dugout canoe under a canopy of thick tropical jungle and along mangrove-lined banks. This traces the route the Caribs followed through the mangrove swamps, from the sea to their settlements.

Cabrits National Park

On the peninsula jutting into the sea between Douglas and Prince Rupert bays stand the ruins of 18th-century **Fort Shirley**. The complex, restored as a museum, contains a hospital, barracks, store-houses, lookout posts and batteries, with a few cannon still facing out to sea. The whole area, endowed with tropical dry woodlands, freshwater swamps, marine reserve and superb recreational opportunities, makes up the Cabrits National Park. An underwater trail marked with white buoys offers excellent snorkelling.

East Coast

The Atlantic coast has a wild, untamed aspect, with beaches of pebbles or black sand, reddish cliffs dropping sheer into the sea and tropical vegetation crowding down to the water's edge.

North and South of Melville Hall

The island's main airport, Melville Hall, lies to the north, linked to Roseau on the west coast by a road cut through the mountain interior. The coastal road from the airport takes you further north to a string of gold-sand beaches, or south through several communities where you can observe fishermen bringing in their catch or mending nets, the villagers building canoes, and bananas and other produce being loaded onto boats.

Carib Territory

Numbering some 3,000, the descendants of the island's original Carib inhabitants now live in a fertile 1,497-ha (3,700-acre) stretch of land running inland from the coast. In three villages, huts with traditionally thatched roofs and plaited walls shelter craft shops where you can buy baskets and other souvenirs made by the Caribs. **Salibia**'s church, where the altar is made from a dug-out canoe, has been restored as a **Carib Museum**.

The fanciful shape of a solidified stream of lava protruding into the sea at **Sineku** has earned it the name Snake Staircase (Escalier Tête Chien) and has inspired some colourful Carib legends. Each rock is inscribed with circles, lines and reptilian scales.

St Lucia

This appealing island midway between Martinique and St Vincent boasts some of the best scenery in the Caribbean—rugged green jungles, undulating agricultural terrain, dazzling beaches and the volcanic, cone-shaped Pitons. There's even a dormant but still bubbling volcano called Soufrière that can be viewed from inside without any danger.

Francophiles love St Lucia for its French atmosphere. Many place-names are French—from the capital, Castries, to Vieux Fort on the southern tip of the island. The official language is English, but most of the 170,000 inhabitants also speak French patois, a remnant of the days of French colonization. Tourism is developing rapidly, but the island remains essentially agricultural, with bananas the main crop. There are provisions for all sorts of summer sports, and you can enjoy good music every night. And indulge in the excellent native cuisine, with its fresh seafood, coconuts, bananas and spicy Creole dishes. Not forgetting the rum.

Castries

The island capital was named in 1785 after Maréchal de Castries, Minister of the Marine responsible for the French colonies. Few buildings remain from the 18th century, mainly due to devastating fires which swept the town in 1948 and 1951. Today's city of around 70,000 inhabitants looks frankly jerrybuilt, though some quarters have retained a certain charm.

Harbour

Take a look at the scenic yacht basin and the lively, ultra-modern **Pointe Seraphine** duty-free shopping complex. Just across the way, the market for food and charcoal, which is used as cooking fuel, hums with activity in the morning. You'll see plenty of island produce for sale, the array varying with the season.

Town Centre

On Bridge Street you'll find the central post office and the largest shops. **Derek Walcott Square**, one of the capital's few picturesque corners, boasts tropical greenery; a saman or rain tree, has been providing shade for four centuries. The square is named after the 1992 Nobel Prize winner for Literature, who has founded a retreat for artists and writers on nearby Rat Island.

The Catholic **cathedral** (19th-century) has wooden columns, iron vaulting and frescoes by a pupil of the French artist Puvis de Chavannes. Opposite stands a red and white structure in stucco and stone, the **Carnegie Library**, surely the most handsome building in town. It also dates from the 19th century but looks much older, and was named after its benefactor, Andrew Carnegie.

Morne Fortuné

The capital is backed by its own mountain, Morne Fortuné, "Lucky Hill". A drive to the top up precipitous roads leads to the 18th-century **Fort Charlotte**, an unremarkable military installation redeemed by spectacular views. Both the French and the British conducted their squabbles from the ramparts.

Three more military buildings were erected on Morne Fortuné in the middle of the 19th century. Restored, they now form part of the island's principal educational complex. But you can still see many reminders of the British and French forces who fought each other for ownership of St Lucia, such as the **Inniskilling Monument** commemorating the British capture of Morne Fortuné in 1796.

Government House, the residence of the Governor General, is an attractive Victorian building on Morne Fortuné, together with St Lucia's small historical museum mainly devoted to colonial times. From this hill you also have a sweeping view of Castries harbour, Vigie peninsula, Pigeon Island and the Pitons.

hemis.fr/Frances

The Petit Piton is one of St Lucia's most spectacular landmarks.

The North

Many of the island's luxury hotels are situated to the north of Castries along a road as good as it is scenic. The hotels are friendly places and they admit non-residents for drinks, meals or a swim. In the area are sparkling crescent-shaped beaches, including Vigie Beach, Choc Beach and Gros Islet.

A short distance inland from Choc Bay, the **Union Nature Trail** includes an interpretive centre and a small zoo with St Lucian parrots.

ST LUCIA FLASHBACK

17th century
Early in the 17th century, a group of Englishmen from a ship called *The Olive Branch* attempts to set up a permanent colony; most are killed by Carib Indians within a few weeks. Efforts by both the British and French to colonize the island prove abortive until the second half of the century.

18th century
Strategically placed, St Lucia continues to tempt the British and French; the island changes hands between them more than a dozen times. In 1765, under the French, the first sugar plantation is started, small towns spring up and the island begins to prosper. But as the repercussions of the American and French revolutions spread to the West Indies, the battle between French and British for Caribbean supremacy intensifies.

19th century
The Treaty of Amiens awards St Lucia to France in 1802. The last transfer of power at the end of the Napoleonic Wars leaves St Lucia in British hands. The 19th century is largely peaceful—an era of coconut, sugar cane, coffee, cacao and cotton plantations. The slaves are emancipated in 1836.

20th century–present
St Lucia heads gradually towards full self-government, finally granted by the West Indies Act of 1967. After a period of mild instability, caused by a tug-of-war between the leading political parties, the island, independent since 1979, returns to its usual state of calm.

istockphoto.com/Geer

Cacao is an important export: here the beans are spread out to dry.

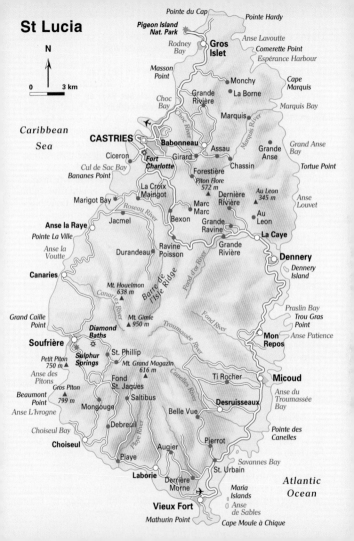

St Lucia

N

0   3 km

Caribbean
Sea

Pointe du Cap
Pointe Hardy
Pigeon Island
Nat. Park
Rodney
Bay
Anse Lavoutte
Gros
Islet
Comerette Point
Espérance Harbour
Masson
Point
Monchy
Cape
Marquis
Grande
Rivière
La Borne
Choc
Bay
Marquis
Marquis Bay
Choc River
Marquis River
CASTRIES
Babonneau
Assau
Grand Anse
Bay
Ciceron
Girard
Grande
Anse
Fort
Charlotte
Chassin
Tortue Point
Forestière
La Croix
Maingot
Piton Flore
572 m
Cul de Sac Bay
Bananes Point
Dernière
Rivière
Au Leon
345 m
Anse
Louvet
Marigot Bay
Marc
Marc
Jacmel
Bexon
Au
Leon
Anse la Raye
Grande
Ravine
La Caye
Pointe La Ville
Ravine
Poisson
Anse la
Voutte
Durandeau
Grande
Rivière
Dennery
Roseau River
Dennery
Island
Canaries
Mt. Houelmon
638 m
Barre de
l'Isle Ridge
Fond d'or River
Grand Caille
Point
Canaries River
Mt. Gimie
950 m
Troumassée River
Praslin Bay
Trou Gras
Point
Fond River
Anse Patience
Diamond
Baths
St. Phillip
Mon
Repos
Soufrière
Sulphur
Springs
Mt. Grand Magazin
616 m
Petit Piton
750 m
Fond
St. Jaques
Ti Rocher
Micoud
Anse des
Pitons
Gros Piton
799 m
Saltibus
Canelles River
Anse du
Troumassée
Bay
Beaumont
Point
Mongouge
Belle Vue
Desruisseaux
Anse L'Ivrogne
Debreuil
Pointe des
Canelles
Choiseul Bay
Piaye River
Augier
Pierrot
Choiseul
Piaye
Savannes Bay
Laborie
Derrière
Morne
St. Urbain
Atlantic
Ocean
Maria
Islands
Vieux Fort
Anse
de Sables
Mathurin Point
Cape Moule à Chique

Pigeon Island

A causeway links Pigeon Island to the mainland. Remarkable for its high, green hill, it is a national park, once the hideout of a French pirate and today the setting for St Lucia's annual Jazz Festival held each May. You can see Martinique to the north. The islet was the main base of Admiral Rodney in the 18th century, and the name probably comes from Rodney's hobby of breeding pigeons. The **Pigeon Island Museum** in the refurbished Officer's Mess traces the island's inhabitants from Amerindians to pirates to whaling men. A multi-media show recreates the 1782 Battle of the Saints in which the British trounced the French and gained control of the Caribbean.

The South

In the 18th century, Maréchal de Laborie established the circular coastal road that skirts the southern two-thirds of the island. You will probably take it to visit St Lucia's most spectacular sights, the Soufrière volcano and the Pitons. Postcards can give no more than an idea of the majesty of these volcanic mountains— **Gros Piton** 799 m (2,619 ft) and **Petit Piton** 750 m (2,460 ft).

If you go by car, it's wise to hire a local driver familiar with all the hair-raising bends, though other alternatives are by boat on a pleasant day's cruise, or on an organized tour.

Bays and Beaches

Just south of Castries, you pass **Cul de Sac Bay**, an aptly named sheltered harbour lined with banana plants. Next comes Marigot Bay, a palm-fringed spot with several hotels and restaurants.

Farther along are more attractive and isolated bays and beaches: **Anse la Raye**, where local people make boats from gum trees and sails from flour bags; **Anse Cochon** (French for pig) and the little fishing village of **Canaries**.

Soufrière

Typically West Indian with its brightly painted arcaded buildings, Soufrière town nestles just under the twin Pitons. It may look unspoiled, but the locals have seen all too many tour groups. Although official guides and the police formally discourage begging, you may be assailed by self-styled guides, their palms held out for money, or little boys who play truant from school to dive for coins.

Follow the road leading to the renovated **Diamond Mineral Baths**, just outside town. The sulphurous springs were discovered by the French, and in 1784, Maréchal de Laborie, then in command of the island, sent samples to Paris.

They were analyzed by Louis XVI's doctors, who pronounced the water to be beneficial. Upon this favourable news, the original baths were constructed.

For a small fee, you can enjoy the same pleasurable steamy effects experienced in de Laborie's day. Botanical gardens and tropical forest make up part of the estate. A path leads to the boiling hot springs, and, beyond, to a lovely waterfall and pond.

Sulphur Springs

From the baths, take the twisting road to Sulphur Springs, advertised as the world's only drive-in volcano. And so it is. The road goes right up to the crater, steaming away like an inferno. Competent guides lead you quickly over the hot stones and through the noxious sulphur gases to an untouchable black pit. Efforts are being made to harness the steam energy for island use. Some of the rocks are coloured green by copper deposits, white by lime and chalk and yellow by sulphur.

In case you're apprehensive, remember that no one ever worries about this dormant volcano erupting violently, since anything that lets off so much steam probably won't blow up for a while. This line of reasoning may not be scientific, but it sounds convincing to anybody who has used a pressure cooker.

Moule à Chique

The road continues southwards passing Choiseul and Laborie, two ramshackle but picturesque little villages. A lighthouse stands on Moule à Chique cape, the island's southernmost point. On a clear day the view from here is spectacular. Out to sea, you'll glimpse the island of St Vincent. The seemingly endless Atlantic beach north of the cape is well whipped by winds and decorated with a glossy hotel.

Dennery

As you travel up the east coast, you'll find the circular road somewhat easier going, not that there isn't plenty to keep a driver alert—children on their way home from school or cows, donkeys and sheep wandering on the road. Headlands project into the ocean, and there are two little towns to explore, Micoud and Dennery. Inland rises **Mt Gimie**, the highest point on the island, 950 m (3,117 ft). Dennery earned renown as a den of iniquity, and until the 1950s a part of town called Oléon (or Aux Lyons) was closed to outsiders. Townspeople made a strong (and illegal) brew known as *mal cochon*, and they were so belligerent in the defense of their privacy that even the police were reluctant to interfere.

From Dennery the road winds back across the island to Castries.

Barbados

The most easterly of the Caribbean islands, Barbados is a coral and limestone-capped isle lying in the path of cooling trade winds. Though the island measures only 34 km by 22 (21 miles by 14), its shores are blessed with almost 100 km (60 miles) of shimmering white strands. The dramatic, windswept east coast is washed by Atlantic waves and dotted with huge boulders, while the tranquil Caribbean beaches of the west coast, edged with palms, are perfect for swimming, snorkelling and sunbathing. Barbados has 280,000 inhabitants, though you're rarely aware of crowds, except on a shopping day in Bridgetown, the capital. Almost sedate in some respects, Bridgetown and Barbados extend a welcome as sunny as the climate. You'll find the Bajans to be warm-hearted and helpful.

Bridgetown

Founded in 1628, the town probably takes its name from an old Indian bridge said to have spanned the River Constitution. The colourful port, with its venerable coral stone mansions, cool green savannahs and lively open-air markets is what one imagines an authentic West Indian capital to be.

Deep Water Harbour

A little out of Bridgetown to the west, the picturesque harbour has its own tourist office and shopping complex, and in the vicinity is the **Pelican Crafts Village**.

East along the wharf lies the **Careenage**—a shallow inlet where boats were beached, or careened, for repair. Fishing boats and pleasure yachts bob cheerfully in the harbour, alongside replicas of pirate ships.

National Heroes Square

The first place to visit in Bridgetown is this bustling plaza at the centre of city activity. In what was known until 1999 as Trafalgar Square, you'll see a dignified bronze monument to Lord Nelson, erected in 1813 (though plans have been made to remove him elsewhere). Although London's famous memorial may be bigger, Bridgetown's was the first—by 30 years! The statue has recently been moved round so Nelson turns his back on Broad Street, a colourful, animated thoroughfare with old colonial buildings. The **Treasury Building** has been hung with portraits of 10 official national heroes, eventually to be replaced by statues.

North of the square, you'll notice the neo-Gothic Public Buildings that have housed the Barbados legislature ever since a fire destroyed most of the neighbourhood in 1860. Roads leading to Swan Street are lined with examples of attractive architecture.

St Michael's Cathedral

Take St Michael's Row to the Anglican Cathedral. It looks like an English parish church, except that it has a red corrugated roof. It was rebuilt in white stone after a hurricane destroyed the original.

Up the road from St Michael's you come to **Queen's Park**, an elegant residence that once housed the British Commanding General. It is now an art gallery, with a small theatre. The adjacent park boasts an enormous baobab, over 18 m (60 ft) in circumference.

Belleville

To the east, this district is a residential area full of pretty Victorian houses, and **Government House**, a mansion dating from the early 18th century and home of the Governor General.

Barbados Museum

The Garrison Savannah, former British military headquarters, lies on the southern outskirts of town. The old military prison houses the Barbados Museum. Scattered over the grassy courtyard is a motley collection of penny-farthings, anchors and sugar moulds. Gallery exhibits highlight local lore, seashells, fish and aspects of the culture of the Arawaks, first inhabitants of the Caribbean. There is a special display of prints relating to the islands, as well as fine English furniture.

hemis.fr/Maisant

Pink sands and foamy surf distinguish the east coast beaches.

St Ann's Fort, nearby, dates from the early years of the 18th century. The fortification, with its conspicuous clock tower, has become a local landmark (no visits).

Atlantic Coast

The rugged Atlantic coast offers some spectacular panoramas. Admire the windswept and dramatic view from **Crane Beach**, where the sea can be rough.

Sam Lord's Castle

The old plantation house, handsomely decorated with grand furniture of Barbados mahogany made locally in the Regency style, is now a hotel and prime tourist attraction. Much of the china and many of the portraits on show are spoils taken from ships wrecked on the rocks offshore by the legendary Sam Lord, who is said to have hung lanterns from the cliffs to lure the ships to their doom on the shallow reef.

BARBADOS FLASHBACK

16th century
Barbados is discovered by Portuguese explorer Pedro a Campos in 1536. He names it los Barbudos ("the bearded ones") after the island's hoary-looking banyan trees, whose hanging roots resemble beards. But Portugal is not particularly interested in Barbados and establishes no permanent outposts there.

17th–18th centuries
An English vessel sails by and claims Barbados for Great Britain in 1625. Englishmen from the ship William and John found Barbados' first settlement, Jamestown (later renamed Holetown), in 1627. Large tobacco, cotton and sugar cane plantations are set up. Thousands of African slaves are introduced to work the fields.

19th century
Both black and white Barbadians enter the new century with optimism as Great Britain ends the slave trade in 1806 and abolishes slavery completely in 1834. But the island passes through hard times, periodic massive destruction from hurricanes and a decline in the value of sugar, the principal cash crop, whose price plummets more than 50% in 50 years.

20th century–present
Great Britain takes steps to improve the economies of its West Indian dependencies, inaugurating an agricultural revolution on Barbados that brings new prosperity. The island begins to diversify its economy, adding sectors such as light industry and tourism. Barbados achieves full independence within the British Commonwealth and joins the United Nations in 1966.

The handsome Garrison Clock Tower at St Ann's Fort.

istockphoto.com/Slattery

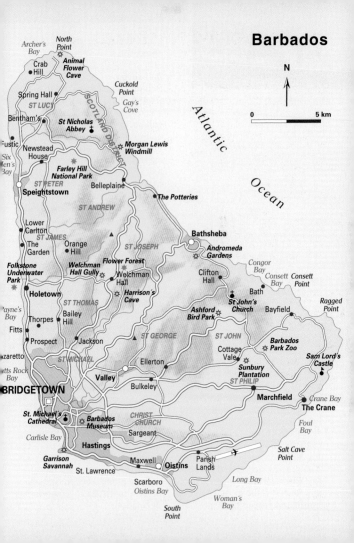

Huber/Mackie

Only one person on the beach at Bottom Bay.

St John

Continue north along the east coast to Conset Bay and the St John area. Villa Nova, a dignified old plantation Great House, is part of a luxury resort, its colonial-style architecture and décor carefully blended with the original stone mansion.

St John's Church, perched 250 m (825 ft) above sea level, offers lovely views of the St John area. The present structure dates back to 1836, and the cemetery, older still, contains the mossy grave of Ferdinando Paleologus, possibly a descendant of the Byzantine emperors.

Bathsheba

Follow the coast road north to the fishing village of Bathsheba, where small pastel houses cling gallantly to chalky cliffs. You can bathe in the whirling waters of the shallow **Bathsheba Pools**, carved from the inshore coral reef. The so-called Soup Bowl nearby is a popular surfing area.

While in the region, be sure to visit the **Andromeda Gardens**, a must on any east coast tour. This botanical garden contains dozens of varieties of indigenous flowers and trees. Among them is the shaggy banyan tree that inspired the name "Barbados".

From Bathsheba the coast road narrows and is dangerous in places, but you'll enjoy the view, especially from the **Potteries** at Chalky Mount, a hilltop craftsmen's village.

Platinum Coast

The west coast takes its name from the brilliant white of its sandy beaches. Many luxury hotels and big private mansions are situated along this "Millionaire's Row". Nevertheless, between the resort developments and imposing estates, you can still see pretty wooden Barbadian houses with their gingerbread decoration.

Holetown

A monument here commemorates the first landing of a British ship on Barbados in 1625. The Anglican **St James's Church**, founded in 1660 and rebuilt in 1874, preserves a 17th-century font.

Speightstown

This was once the sugar capital of the northwest area. The town was known as "Little Bristol", since the Speight family made most of their trade with the English port. Speightstown has remained typically West Indian, with small, pastel wooden houses and shops, old churches and an easygoing populace greeting one another in the streets.

Just north at **Six Men's Bay**, old cannon are ranged about the silvery shore, another picturesque reminder of the past, and fishing boats bob in the surf.

North Point

At the northern tip of the island is **Animal Flower Cave**, where a guide will lead you down steep steps to a cavern carved out by the sea. You'll see the animal flower itself—an exquisite sea anemone. High waves occasionally close the caves.

Plantation Houses

On the return journey, take the road that winds through St Lucy Parish to **Farley Hill**, once a venerable plantation house. Many royal visitors were entertained here, including King George V, and the house was the setting for the film *Island in the Sun*. A fire damaged the building and the government finally took over the property.

St Nicholas Abbey, another plantation house, is one of the oldest in the Caribbean, built around 1650 in Jacobean style with Dutch gables. A short distance east stands the restored **Morgan Lewis Windmill**, a reminder of the days when sugarmaking was introduced by Dutch settlers from Brazil.

Welchman Hall

On your way back to Bridgetown, across the island, take a walk through Welchman Hall Gully. This deep, wide ravine was planted with citrus and spices in the 19th century but left to grow wild until developed as an island attraction in the 1960s. In nearby **Harrison's Cave**, a tram will take you through a cavern of stalagmites and stalactites.

Flower Forest

Another botanical showplace is **Richmond Plantation**. Splendid views of the sea and the Scotland district compete with horticultural attractions from ginger lilies to cabbage palms.

THE MOON

Post Office

OFFICE

YACHT CLUB

SUPER MARKET

Immigration

P S V RESORT

CHARTER FLIGHT

Palm Island

CUSTOMS

Hotel

All you need is close at hand in the
Grenadines.

Restaurant

hemis.fr

St Vincent and the Grenadines

St Vincent surges from the sea like a comet, capped by a simmering volcano and trailing a tail of islets in its wake—the glistening Grenadines. Constant and intense volcanic activity through the ages has endowed St Vincent with a fringe of shiny black-sand beaches, notably on the Atlantic side. Yet the bleakly spectacular coast can melt into lush terraced hills a few miles inland, and in the south the beaches are golden coral. La Soufrière, an active volcano, dominates the island's entire northern end.

Nature has been kind to St Vincent's 118,000 inhabitants. Bananas, coconuts, cacao and yams all flourish on the "Breadfruit Island"—it was the first in the Caribbean to be planted with the fruit brought from the South Pacific by the legendary Captain Bligh. St Vincent has long been a great producer of arrowroot, and it also grows Sea Island cotton, one of the softest natural fibres in the world. There's something here for everyone.

Kingstown
St Vincent's unassuming capital lies on a sheltered bay. Its streets are lined with arcades, many of them left over from French colonial times.

Harbour
In sight of Mount St Andrew and Dorsetshire Hill, the harbour is always alive with schooners and fishing boats, and the business of loading island produce. Kingstown's food market ranks among the best in the Caribbean, especially on weekend mornings. Shops are situated near the seaport and market.

Churches
In Grenville Street, towards the other end of town, you'll see an ecumenical trio: St George's Anglican Cathedral, the Methodist Church, and St Mary's Roman Catholic Church. This last, a fanciful pot-pourri of Romanesque, Gothic and Renaissance styles, would delight any storybook illustrator. There are towers, crosses and fret-work all over, and the courtyards are situated in odd places. Surprisingly, it's a recent construction, restored in the 1930s by Benedictine monks from Trinidad.

Botanic Gardens
Said to be the oldest in the western hemisphere, the Botanic Gardens were founded in 1765. They are situated just below the Governor's Residence.

Fort Charlotte
Just west of Kingstown, the fort merits a visit for the view, if

ST VINCENT AND THE GRENADINES FLASHBACK

15th–17th centuries
Columbus discovers St Vincent in 1498. The Carib Indians fiercely resist British and French attempts to colonize the island. The Grenadines come under a Norman feudal lord, Jacques Diel du Parquet. Escaped and ship-wrecked African slaves begin intermarrying with the natives towards the end of the 17th century, creating a new race, the Black Caribs.

18th century
St Vincent passes back and forth between the British and French. In 1795, the islanders side with the French against the British colonizers in the Brigands' War, but the British overcome the opposition and banish over 5,000 troublemakers from Bequia (mostly Carib Indians) to Honduras. This time Britannia rules for nearly two centuries.

19th century–present
Britain outlaws slave-trading throughout its colonies in 1807 and slavery itself in 1833. Indentured labourers are brought in a few years later from Portugal and India to work the cane fields. Future King George V and his brother Prince Alfred visit the Grenadines in 1880. St Vincent and Grenada both become British Associate States in the 1960s but then gain independence in the 1970s. The Grenadines are split up between Grenada and St Vincent, with the dividing line on the northern extremity of Carriacou. Yachtsmen, and then tourists, discover the Grenadines. In 2009 the people vote to remain within the Commonwealth.

hemis.fr/Gardel

nothing else. Take a panoramic look at the capital, harbour and nearby Grenadines through the handy telescope erected at the top. The fort was built by the British as a defence against the French and named after the wife of King George III. Three of the original cannon are still in place, and the lookout point is used for monitoring ships.

The austere former barracks building now serves as a museum displaying colourful contemporary paintings by William Linze Prescott. The canvases depict some rather lurid scenes from St Vincent's history.

The **Women's Prison**, a short distance downhill, looks out on one of the loveliest views in the world.

Dorsetshire Hill

For more views of Kingstown and the harbour, climb east of the city up to Dorsetshire Hill, taking the twisting road starting

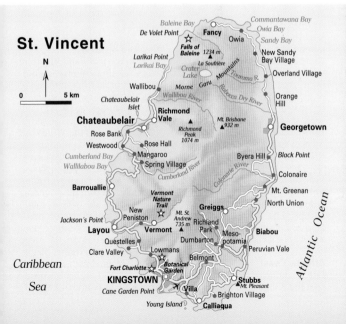

St. Vincent

N

0   5 km

Baleine Bay
De Volet Point
Commantawana Bay
Owia Bay
Fancy
Owia
Sandy Bay
Falls of Baleine
1234 m
La Soufrière
New Sandy Bay Village
Larikai Point
Larikai Bay
Crater Lake
Morne Garu Mountains
Wamanu R.
Overland Village
Wallibou
Morne Garu
Orange Hill
Chateaubelair Islet
Wallibou River
Rabacca Dry River
Richmond Vale
Mt Brisbane 932 m
Georgetown
Chateaubelair
Richmond Peak 1074 m
Rose Bank
Westwood
Rose Hall
Cumberland Bay
Mangaroo
Spring Village
Byera Hill
Black Point
Wallilabou Bay
Cumberland River
Colonaire River
Colonaire
Mt. Greenan
Barrouallie
Vermont Nature Trail
North Union
New Peniston
Mt. St Andrew 735 m
Greiggs
Jackson's Point
Richland Park
Biabou
Layou
Vermont
Mesopotamia
Questelles
Lowmans
Dumbarton
Peruvian Vale
Clare Valley
Belmont
Botanical Garden
Caribbean Sea
Fort Charlotte
KINGSTOWN
Stubbs
Mt. Pleasant
Cane Garden Point
Villa
Brighton Village
Young Island
Calliaqua
Atlantic Ocean

from Sion Hill near Arnos Vale airport.

Caribbean Coast

From Kingstown, drive north-west via the Leeward Highway, the name for the narrow road that twists its way along the coast. As you travel northwards, you come upon one stunning sea view after another, and in between there are small towns like Questelles, a community of primitive houses and neat churches.

Petroglyphs

Just before the small fishing village of Layou Bay, stop to admire the Indian petroglyphs, stone carvings estimated to be at least 1,400 years old. They are on a large boulder in a private property so you need permission to inspect them. More can be seen in the school grounds at Barrouallie, a whaling village 5 km (3 miles) further along the road.

Richmond Beach

Some 30 miles (48 km) from Kingstown, the road comes to an abrupt end near Richmond Beach, a deserted place ideal for a picnic or swim.

Atlantic Coast

Drive southeast along the coast past the Kingstown airport. You travel through the town's main residential and hotel district into suburbs where English-style lawns surround large villas.

Young Island

This private island has been developed as a luxury resort, but non-residents can cross over on the hotel boat to enjoy a drink or a meal and explore the grounds. For a small fee, you'll be permitted to use the pool or the small beach. **Fort Duvernette**, on an adjacent islet reputed to have figured in battles with the Caribs, is now the scene of torch-lit barbecue suppers.

Windward Highway

Back on the mainland, the road enters farming country, including land broken up into small plots planted with peanuts, yams, potatoes, cassava and corn.

Now known as the Windward Highway, the road parallels the shimmering volcanic black-sand beaches of the Atlantic coast. Stop at **Mount Pleasant** for an impressive view of the pounding surf. But beware: winds, rough water and sharp rocks make swimming in the Atlantic dangerous. Farther along, the green Argyle district—a former plantation still planted with arrowroot, coconuts and other crops—extends up to Peruvian Vale.

From here to the village of Georgetown, you drive through more rugged Atlantic scenery. From Georgetown, a poor road leads to **Rabacca Dry River**, a region marked by former volcanic activity. You'll need a jeep to continue on to Fancy, a village at the northern tip of the island.

Mesopotamia

Inland, the Mesopotamia district, otherwise known as the Marri-aqua Valley, is one of the island's most picturesque regions. **Belvedere Point** looks out over this agricultural area. Green, richly cultivated fields climb neatly terraced hillsides interspersed with pretty villages. Every inch is planted with peanuts, nutmeg, bananas and plantain.

La Soufrière

This full day's excursion for the very hardy is best attempted on an organized tour. Starting out early in the morning, you travel by car, switching to a land-rover which carries you over dirt roads to the vicinity of the crater. The climb up takes 2 to 3 hours — through hot (and sometimes rainy) jungle territory, but with plenty of rewarding plant and bird life to be seen.

La Soufrière's biggest eruption occurred between March and May, 1902, when at least 2,000 inhabitants were killed. A

istockphoto.com/Alia

istockphoto.com/Tilghman

Banana blossom: purple bracts protecting the male flowers. | An adolescent green sea turtle.

beautiful crater lake was created. Minor explosions in 1970 and 1971 gave birth to a lava dome which formed an island in the centre of the lake. But this was destroyed by the gas-and-ash eruption of April, 1979.

If you climb to the top of the crater today, you'll find a mass of whitish-grey hot ash in place of the one-time lake and island. Though walking is arduous, the excursion shouldn't be dangerous, as the volcano is constantly monitored.

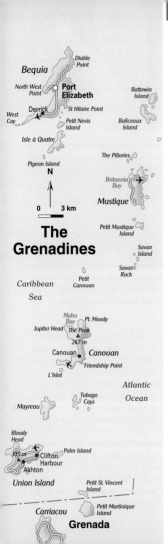

Bequia

Diable Point

North West Point

Port Elizabeth

Derrick

West Cay

St Hilaire Point

Petit Nevis Island

Battowia Island

Balliceaux Island

Isle à Quatre

The Pillories

Pigeon Island

N

Britannia Bay

Mustique

0   3 km

Petit Mustique Island

The Grenadines

Savan Island

Savan Rock

Caribbean Sea

Petit Canouan

Maho Bay   Pt. Moody

Jupiter Head   The Peak
                267 m

Canouan   **Canouan**

L. Islot   Friendship Point

Atlantic Ocean

Mayreau

Tobago Cays

Bloody Head

305 m   Palm Island

Clifton Harbour

Ashton

Union Island

Petit St. Vincent Island

Petit Martinique Island

Carriacou

Grenada

The Grenadines

So remote are these islands that opinions differ as to just how many there are. Counting all the islets and rocky outcrops, some only a few yards across, they total around 600, of which some 125 constitute the core of the Grenadines. Some are rich in vegetation, with sheltered harbours and coves offering exceptional sailing and sunbathing. Others are rocky and uninhabited, protected from "invasion" by sheer, breathtaking cliffs. They are so close together that, whichever one you are on, there is always another in sight.

Bequia

The small, tidily developed island lies just 15 km (9 miles) from mainland St Vincent. Visitors arrive at J.F. Mitchell Airport or—more colourfully perhaps—in Admiralty Bay. On the beach, fishermen mend their nets and hand-build their boats, maintaining age-old traditions and Bequia's most important industry.

The quaint waterfront at Port Elizabeth is lined with bars, restaurants and shops. There's also a tourist board near the dock that will help you fix inland tours and can arrange cars and drivers by the day.

The main sights on Bequia can be covered in half a day: **Old Fort** affords a good view of Admiralty

Bay; **Paget Farm** is a quaint whaling village (whaling with hand-thrown harpoons is still practised in the Grenadines); **Vista Point** offers views of St Vincent and other Grenadine islands; there are a couple of hotels at **Friendship Bay**; **Moon Hole**, a troglodytic residential development, has literally been carved from the cliffs. **Princess Margaret Bay** is noted for its coral reef and excellent snorkelling. Because the road is poor, it's best to go there by boat. An inexpensive water taxi service is available from Port Elizabeth.

Mustique

The name comes from the French word for mosquito, but this shouldn't put you off. After all, the green and hilly island has not deterred some of the world's richest and most famous people—Mick Jagger, David Bowie, Raquel Welch and many more—from building impressive villas on this privately owned island. Princess Margaret was given a plot of land as a wedding present; she adored staying here, but when she gave her holiday home, Jolies Eaux, to her son Viscount Linley he promptly sold it, much to her chagrin. For all its publicity, Mustique has remained secluded, and looks more like a desert isle than a gathering place for the jet set.

Unless you rent one of the villas or are the guest of someone who owns one, you are unlikely to go further than the sandy beaches and turquoise waters of **Britannia Bay**, a famous yachtsmen's and sailors' haunt. The exception is the island's only hotel, **Cotton House**, a sprawling 18th-century plantation house designed by Oliver Messel. This luxurious establishment bears all the hallmarks of rustic elegance, with louvered windows, Spanish silver screens and a fountain of scallop shells.

Canouan

Canouan claims some of the best beaches in the Caribbean. Long hot ribbons of powdery white sands blend with warm clear water and coral. The 2000 inhabitants are mostly farmers and fishermen. The island has been developed as a discreet resort, with a few hotels and guest houses already constructed.

Tobago Cays

The cays are four uninhabited islets surrounded by truly spectacular coral reefs. This wildlife reserve is the perfect paradise for escapists. There is sailing, snorkelling, swimming and picnicking in complete seclusion—a rare tropical Eden, normally reached by chartered yacht or a daily connection from Union Island.

Mayreau

Tiny Mayreau has no roads and a small local population. On the highest hill, the single village snuggles round a delightful little church, built by a French family in the early 1800s and still a Sunday gathering place for the island's inhabitants. Salt Whistle Bay harbours the island's only hotel. The beach here is one of the most sheltered in the Grenadines, perfect for children.

Union Island

Here you're almost back to civilization! There's an airport, a bank and even a small hospital. But don't worry, as elsewhere in the Grenadines, the main charm is sheer escapism. The island's silhouette is quite distinctive, with the impressive Mount Parnassus, "the Pinnacle", soaring from the sea. Clifton Harbour, the main town, is small but commercial.

Palm Island

Privately owned, the flat, 45-ha island was named for the coconut palms lining its white-sand beaches. A resort-hotel, it offers every kind of water sport and tennis. Life here is casual but chic.

Petit St Vincent

The southernmost St Vincent Grenadine, Petit St Vincent (PSV), is also privately owned but is more hilly than its neighbour Palm. The simple seclusion and carefree lifestyle makes this one a favourite with yachtsmen.

Underwater Wonderland. A host of exotic creatures inhabits the watery depths of the Caribbean. Apart from beautiful flower-like sea anemones, common sights include elkhorn, finger and brain coral, which look exactly as their names imply. In addition, you may see fire and pillar coral, as well as sea fans. Take care not to step on the razor-sharp coral, and refrain from touching their fragile formations. Slow to grow and easily damaged, coral reefs are formed by tiny animals called polyps which live in surface cavities and feed on plankton.

Fish are not all shy about parading their gorgeous colours past snorkellers and divers. Look for the bright-blue-and-yellow Queen Angelfish, the orange-and-blue Honeytail Damselfish and striking Queen Triggerfish. The blue Ocean Surgeon has a neat "incision" marked in black on its gill, and the Sergeant-Major sports pretty blue, yellow and black stripes.

Corbis/Westmorland

Grenada

Spice is a way of life in Grenada. One of the most southerly of the Caribbean chain, it is the only major spice-growing island in the western hemisphere, producing a fifth of the world's supply of nutmeg, as well as cinnamon, cloves, bay leaves, saffron and mace. Even the breeze is heady with their fragrance.

The vibrant lifestyle of Grenada's 107,000 inhabitants matches the luxuriance of the island's natural assets. Dense carpets of tropical rainforest drape the volcanic mountains in a tangle of coconut palms, lianas and flowering shrubs. Waterfalls cascade down the hillsides to groves of nutmeg nestling in the valleys.

Grenada's largest neighbours are Trinidad and Tobago, 145 km (90 miles) to the south. To the north lie the tiny Grenadines, of which Carriacou, Petit-Martinique and several islets belong to Grenada.

St George's

Built on hills surrounding the blue lagoon of its inner harbour, St George's, Grenada's tiny capital and chief port, with a population of around 100,000, is often acclaimed as the world's most picturesque. The mellowed bricks, wrought-iron balconies and red-tiled roofs of English Georgian and French provincial houses preserve the flavour of its colonial past.

Carenage

Along the Carenage, the curving waterfront of the inner harbour, attractive 18th-century warehouses line the quay. High on a hill overlooking the harbour stands **Fort George**, erected by the French in 1705. From here it's a short distance to the **Botanical Gardens**, majestically heralded by a clump of royal palms. The gardens bloom with an array of tropical flowers, and you may sight some brilliantly plumed Caribbean birds.

Town Centre

Sendall Tunnel leads from the Carenage to the Outer Harbour and Melville Street, a shopping centre on the quayside. One street inland, **Market Square** is the site of a typical West Indian open-air market. Among the wares for sale in the area are all manner of straw goods, carvings and paintings, as well as a profusion of local spices. On Church Street, the clock tower of the Anglican Church has become something of a town symbol, as has that of the Presbyterian Kirk.

Fort Frederick

Up on Richmond Hill, the fort is a splendid lookout point. Con-

GRENADA FLASHBACK

Pre-Columbian era

By AD 300, the Arawak Indians from South America have settled throughout the Caribbean. They are driven out by the warlike Caribs, also from South America.

15th–17th centuries

In 1498, Columbus discovers Grenada on his third voyage. It is inhabited by warlike Caribs, who drove out the Arawaks, an Indian tribe that settled throughout the Caribbean before ad 300. Columbus calls the island Concepción, but later Spanish sailors rename it after their native Granada. Early attempts by both British and French to subdue the Caribs fail, and it is not until 1650 that the French establish a foothold. They carry out a campaign of extermination against the Caribs. When defeat is certain, the last small group of Indians jump to their deaths from a northern cliff. Slaves are brought in to work the sugar plantations.

18th century

The British oust the French from Grenada in 1762 but are driven out in 1779. France holds the island for four years, until the Treaty of Versailles (1783) awards it to Britain. In 1795, a slave uprising provokes bloody reprisals.

19th century

Slavery is abolished in all British colonies in 1834. Contract workers from India and Africa begin arriving to replace slave labour on the Caribbean plantations. In 1843, nutmeg is introduced to Grenada from the Dutch East Indies and soon takes over from sugar as the island's principal export. Grenada is formally declared a Crown Colony of Britain in 1877.

20th century–present

An elected legislature is created in 1924 and the island is made a British Associated State in 1967. Grenada achieves full independence in 1974 but remains within the British Commonwealth. A coup d'état in the spring of 1979 deposes Prime Minister Sir Eric Gairy and installs Maurice Bishop at the head of a People's Revolutionary Government. In the autumn of 1983, Maurice Bishop is killed during an attempted takeover by the extremist elements of his own party. Cuban involvement precipitates military intervention by the United States; the US forces leave in 1985. Today the economy is based on agriculture and tourism.

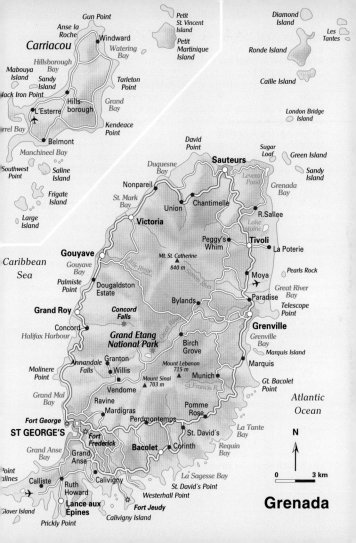

Grenada

struction was begun by the French in 1779, but it was the British who applied the finishing touches in 1783.

South

Heading south from St George's, the **Royal Drive** was named in honour of Queen Elizabeth. You'll probably want to stop on the way at **Morne Jaloux Ridge** to admire views considered fit for a queen. The road winds at first through green hills (known as mornes in the West Indies) past neat little settlements and farming country. As you approach the deeply indented southern coastline, the landscape grows wilder and more desolate, until finally you reach Fort Jeudy, where black volcanic rock rears out of a surging sea.

Beaches

From **Point Salines**, on the southwest tip of the island, sandy beaches stretch northwards along the Caribbean coast. One of them, **Grand Anse Beach**, has gained renown for the shimmering silvery whiteness of its 3-km (2-mile) expanse.

North

The scenic route to the northern spice plantations follows the west coast, with bays and headlands of uncommon beauty. You'll see wooden huts, brightly painted boats and long seine nets hanging out to dry in some of the prettiest fishing villages in the Caribbean.

Gouyave

Hidden among the red roofs of Gouyave (formerly Charlotte Town) is a factory where spices are sorted and dried in preparation for shipping all over the world. Chief among factory products are nutmeg and the mace made from its filament.

To see spices growing on a traditional plantation, head inland for a short distance to **Dougaldston Estate**, a centre for the cultivation of nutmeg and cacao.

Northern Tip

Near the village of Sauteurs is **Morne des Sauteurs** (Leaper's Hill), the rocks from which the last of the Carib Indians plummeted to death in 1650 rather than surrender to the French. The cliff is not as spectacular as one would imagine, but the rocks about 12 m (40 ft) below look sufficiently sinister. Just east lies **Levera Bay** and its beach. Columbus reputedly spotted this very place as he sailed past the island in 1498. In nearby **Levera National Park**, sea turtles nest on pristine beaches and mangroves harbour a large variety of birds.

Grenville

On the eastern coast, Grenada's third-largest town seems more like a casual village. It does have a lively market, however, and its own spice factory. South of Grenville, the once-hidden Carmel Waterfall is now accessible by walking trail.

Grand-Etang National Park

The inland road returning to St George's is simply spectacular. Numerous hairpin bends take you through tropical rainforests and past gorges of exceptional beauty. The road passes within hailing distance of Grand Etang National Park and its extinct volcano, alt. 549 m (1,800 ft), cradling a lake that covers 12 ha (30 acres).

Carriacou

An island of green hills and sandy beaches, Carriacou is the largest of the Grenadines and lies 37 km (23 miles) northeast of Grenada. The 6,500-strong population has French, Scottish and African origins: these last are celebrated in the Big Drum Dances which take place around Easter.

Hillsborough

In the capital (population 800), seek out the interesting Carriacou Historical Society Museum on Paterson Street, which displays exhibits from Amerindian settlements, including interesting pre-Columbian pottery.

To the northeast of town, climb **Hospital Hill** for splendid views.

Tyrrel Bay

A Glaswegian shipbuilder introduced his craft to the island. At Tyrrel Bay you can watch the men at work beneath the coconut palms, using white cedar imported from Grenada to make sturdy schooners without the use of power tools. Many yachts call in here, and there are oyster beds where tree-oysters grow on mangrove roots.

Anse la Roche

On the northwest coast, this fine, isolated beach is best reached by water taxi. There are no facilities, so take a picnic. You can walk from here to **Gun Point**, the island's northern tip, and Petit Carenage Bay with coral sand. A little further down the east coast, Windward was settled mainly by Scotsmen.

Petit-Martinique

If you really want to get away from it all, hop onto the cargo ship that links Hillsborough twice a week with Petit-Martinique, a tiny dot of an island 5 km (3 miles) to the northeast. The 600 inhabitants live mainly from fishing. There is one guesthouse, one church and one road, but most people prefer to walk.

During Trinidad's Carnival, thousands of revellers dance in the streets.

hemis.fr / Garde

Trinidad

Take a Caribbean island endowed with rich natural resources and lush scenery, people it with a variety of nationalities and faiths, add the calypso and the steel-band sound, and there you have a thumbnail sketch of Trinidad. The island covers a large area of 4,828 sq km (1,864 sq miles), or about 80 by 56 km (50 by 35 miles). In some distant geological age, it probably broke away from Venezuela, some 11 km (7 miles) to the south, a theory given some credibility by striking similarities between the two in rock formation, flora and fauna. Together with its small neighbour Tobago, much the opposite in atmosphere and character, it forms the Republic of Trinidad and Tobago, with Port of Spain as its capital.

Port of Spain

Verdant hills surround the capital, and the people live in everything from shacks to imposing colonial mansions. The architecture embraces a variety of styles from neo-Gothic to glossy contemporary, and the restaurants vary from French to fast food and *roti* stands. Port of Spain is dotted with parks of all shapes and sizes, which Trinis like to compare to those of London. But the similarity between England and Trinidad begins and ends with cricket, and you'll never doubt for a moment that you're in the tropics.

Frederick Street

Lined with shops, this main thoroughfare runs from Independence Square, a short walk from the modern cruise terminal, north to Queen's Park Savannah. Street vendors congregate at the lower end. The square, laid out by the Spanish as a military parade ground, serves as an assembly point for participants in carnival parades. The Catholic **Cathedral of the Immaculate Conception** is a simple bluestone structure of 1832, renovated in 1984, with two bell towers and a vaulted interior.

Woodford Square

Heading north, you come to a large green space in the centre of town, site of the stately parliament building, the **Red House**, and the neo-Gothic Anglican **Cathedral of the Holy Trinity**, with its beautifully carved mahogany altar and choir stalls.

Queen's Park Savannah

This vast expanse of greenery boasts a racecourse, playing fields and plenty of food stands. On the south side stands the **National Museum and Art Gallery**, interesting for its displays of Amerindian relics and carnival costumes.

Magnificent Seven

North along Maraval Road lies an amazing collection of old mansions known as the **Magnificent**

TRINIDAD AND TOBAGO FLASHBACK

15th–16th centuries

Columbus sights Trinidad on his third voyage in 1498. It is inhabited by Caribs. Spain founds a colony in 1532 but uses it mainly as a base from which to search for the gold of El Dorado. In 1598 Sir Walter Raleigh burns down the newly founded Spanish town of San José and discovers Pitch Lake.

17th–18th centuries

The English attempt to settle Tobago, but disease and Carib raids decimate the inhabitants. The Dutch invade in 1658, then English privateers take over (1666), followed the next year by the French, and so on, changing hands dozens of times. African slaves are imported to work in the plantations on both islands. Tobago is declared neutral territory in 1748, but Anglo-French rivalry intensifies. Around 1770, when the first slave uprising occurs, there are 3,000 African inhabitants and only 200 whites. From 1781 the French hold sway, but the British regain control in 1793. In 1783, a Spanish royal proclamation calls upon Catholics of all nationalities to settle on Trinidad. The British capture Trinidad in 1797, but Spain does not concede ownership until 1802.

19th century

Tobago changes hands between Britain and France until 1814, when the British are back to stay. Slavery is abolished in 1833 and the former slaves move inland to set up small farms. Thousands of indentured labourers from India and the Far East are recruited to replace the slave work force. Sugar, cotton and rum production flourish. Tobago becomes a Crown Colony in 1877, but prosperity ends abruptly in 1884 with the collapse of the sugar market. Five years later Tobago is joined to Trinidad.

20th century–present

Oil is discovered on Trinidad. During World War II the US builds bases on Trinidad to protect the Caribbean. The two islands gain independence in 1962. In 1976 Trinidad-Tobago becomes a republic, remaining within the Commonwealth, with a president as Head of State. Tobago has a separate House of Assembly. Oil plays a dominant role in the economy.

Caribbean Sea

Atlantic Ocean

Trinidad

Galera Pt.

Sans Souci Bay
Sans Souci
Toco
Redhead
Rampanalgas
Grande Riviere
Matelot
Balandra Bay
Matura Pt.
Point Radix

Grande Riviere Bay
Grand Matelot Pt.
Salibea
Matura National Park
Matura
Matura Bay

Chupara Pt.
Chupara Bay
Filette
Blanchisseuse
Las Cuevas
Paria Falls
Madamas National Park
El Cerro del Aripo
936 m
940 m

Maracas Bay
La Vache Pt.
Las Cuevas Bay
ASA Wright Nature Center
Mt. Tucuche
Monastery
St. Benedict
Tacarigua
Arouca
Tunapuna
Maracas
St. Joseph
Maraval
San Juan
St. Augustine
El Socorro
Barataria
PORT OF SPAIN
St. Peter's Bay

Cantaro
Loopinet
Dinsley
Cunupia
Caroni Bird Sanctuary
Caroni Swamp National Park

Valencia
San Raphael
Talparo
Mundo Nuevo
Flanagin Town
Longdenville
Cumuto
Brickfield
Tabaquite
Gran Couva
Chaguanas
Waterloo
Couva
California

Sangre Grande
Mount Harris
Upper Manmanzanilla
Lower Manzanilla
Manzanilla Bay
Cocos Bay
St. Joseph
Pierreville
Navara Bay
Guayaguayare
Galeota Pt.

Nariva Swamp
Cumoto
Nestor
Mamon
Biche
Chuma
Rio Claro
Poole
Indian Walk
St. Julien Tableland
St. Croix
Cipero
Sante Croix
Debe
Penal
Sipario
Palo Seco
Guayaguayare Bay
Guayaguayare

Mt. Tamana
308 m
Novet
Mc Dom
Navet
Trinity Hills
304 m
Basse Terre
Preau
Moruga

Gasparillo
Princess Town
Bird Sanctuary Wild Fowl Trust
Marabella
San Fernando
Pointe-à-Pierre
Congrejos Pt.
Lisas Bay
Pt. Lisas

Rich Lake
La Brea
Pitch Pt.
Guapo Bay
Point Fortin
Irois Bay

Fyzabad
Parrylands
Buenos Ayres
San Francique

Corozal Pt.
Green Hill
Blue Bassin
Chaguaramas
Chaguaramas National Park
Gaspar Grande
Monos
Huevos
Chacachacare
Entrada Pt.

Golfo de Paria

Moruga Pt.
Erin Pt.
Palo Seco Bay
St. Mary's
Chatham
Granville
Bonasse
Cedros Pt.
Cedros
Fullarton
Icacos Pt.
Islote Bay
Isiote Pt.

N

20 km

0

istockphoto.com/Pershern

Tiny frangipani flowers fill the air with their fragrance.

Seven. Here lived the cream of Trinidad society. **Roodal's House**, sometimes referred to as Roomor, is decorated in a frothy Creole style that belies its description of "French Second Empire". **White Hall**, a Moorish-style structure, once served as the Prime Minister's office. **Stollmeyers Castle** (also known as Killarney), a white elephant of a house, belonged to a German family. This turreted, crenellated stone affair has been bought and restored by the government but is presently standing empty.

Emperor Valley Zoo

On the northern side of the Savannah, the zoo contains chimpanzees and colourful birds, as well as misleadingly benign-looking cayman alligators and restlessly pacing ocelots. It was named for Trinidad's black-and-turquoise Emperor butterflies. But the **Royal Botanic Gardens** next door are one of the town's major attractions. You'll see everything from frangipani and sausage trees to the raw beef tree, which seems to bleed when a cut is made in the bark. Adjoining the garden is the **President's Palace**, formerly the Governor General's residence, a Caribbean version of the neo-Renaissance.

Fort George

You'll want to admire the view of town from Fort George, on the outskirts. The small house at the top of the fort overlooks the whole of Paria Bay. On a clear day you can see all the way to Venezuela from this 334-m (1,100-ft) vantage point.

Island Sights

Tourist offices organize circular tours of the island, taking about eight hours.

Caroni Bird Sanctuary

About 11 km (7 miles) southeast of Port of Spain, the sanctuary has magnificent blue and white herons and other exotic water-birds nesting in its mangrove swamps, but the climax of the tour is at sunset when hundreds of scarlet ibis fill the sky with the flutter of their flame-coloured feathers.

Chaguaramas Peninsula

Part of a national park, the peninsula is dominated by 540-m (1,768-ft) Mount Catherine. The island of Gaspar Grande has interesting caves.

hemis.fr/Frilet

Carnival and Calypso. French settlers first brought to the Caribbean the custom of carnival, which has developed in Trinidad to something of an art form, and is the biggest event of the year. The Spaniards added their own inspiration, and, after emancipation in 1834, freed slaves brought new rhythms and music, imaginative instruments made from bamboo, gourds, bottles and pans. Today, tension and excitement build up in the weeks preceding carnival in Port of Spain as everyone prepares for the big event, which is limited to just 43 hours, from 5 a.m. Monday to midnight on Shrove Tuesday. The festivities open with the crowning of the Carnival King, then the first big bands shuffle into Independence Square. By Monday afternoon, everyone is dancing to the music as more costumed bands parade, and in the evening, celebrations are in full swing, helped along by generous quantities of rum. The final day of parades takes place at Queen's Park Savannah, a mind-boggling spectacle of light, sound and colour.

The steel band, a musical way of life all over the Caribbean, originated in Trinidad in 1937, when a group marched into Port of Spain during a carnival parade banging out a melody on old oil drums. The sound soon caught on, with a "pan tuner" today commanding great respect. The metal is tempered by heat, then hammered, the tuner making indentations that make different sounds when struck with mallets. The Trinis also take credit for inventing the calypso, which may have its origins in a West African dance chorus. The music combines slave songs and African rhythms with French, Spanish, Irish, even Chinese and Indian elements, a sound-picture of this unique island heritage, which you'll also notice in its architecture, food and population.

The red ibis: a sacred bird and a national symbol.

Maracas Beach
The panoramic north-coast road, the Skyline Highway, takes you to one of the most popular swimming areas on Trinidad, a circular bay with clean white sand and good surfing. Lifeguards are on duty, and facilities include changing rooms. Snacks (such as deep-fried battered shark) and drinks are available. On Sundays and public holidays it seems as though the entire island population has gathered here for one big beach party. The bay boasts the island's only beach-front hotel.

Lopinot
Established by a French nobleman fleeing the Revolution, the cacao estate in the mountains near Arima gives a fascinating glimpse into the life of a 19th-century planter. A river tumbles through the groves and the views are idyllic. **Arima** has a small museum of Indian artefacts and a craft centre.

Asa Wright Nature Centre
The state-sponsored scientific foundation lies about an hour's drive east of Port of Spain. Visitors are welcome to join the bird-watchers, entomologists and botanists who assemble here to study the flora and fauna of Trinidad. Many people come just to catch a glimpse of the rare oil bird or guacharo that inhabits the caves in the grounds.

Chaguanas
This little town, about 72 km (45 miles) southeast of Port of Spain, makes a good stop in the morning when the food market is in full swing.

Pitch Lake
In the southwest of the island, at La Brea, Pitch Lake was discovered by Sir Walter Raleigh. This heaving black patch of asphalt is created by crude oil, seeping up from the interior through a fault in the sandstone.

Tobago

Tobago takes its name from the tobacco plant, or from the Spanish name for the natives' pipes. The 60,000 Tobagonians like to cultivate their difference from the people of nearby Trinidad. Most of its citizens (90 per cent, in fact) are descendants of black slaves, and there is nothing resembling the multiracial mix of the larger island. The folklore, religion and food all find their roots in Africa. Nearly all of Tobago's 42 by 11 km (26 by 7 miles) provides perfect scenery and relaxation. Construction and development of the tourist infrastructure has brought some change to the island, but it has retained much of its primitive aspect and charm.

Scarborough

Tobago's capital is a sleepy little town of some 4,700. Built on two levels, it clusters around a modern harbour. There is not much in the way of sightseeing; most visitors head straight up to the fort.

Fort King George

The islands principal sight, the fort was completed in 1779. It stands high above the town. From here you can see neighbouring Bacolet and beyond, across the Atlantic, to Trinidad.

The fort bears witness to French-British rivalry for the island, and a plaque commemo-

rates all the changes in its fortune: France 1781, Great Britain 1793, and so on. A bronze cannon from the George III period remains in place, and there are plenty of exotic plants to admire, especially in the peaceful garden of a ruined church on the site. There's also a small historical and archaeological museum housing a collection of antique charts and Amerindian and colonial artefacts.

Tobago's hospital and former prison are situated downhill from the fort. The once formidable prison was the scene of a revolt in 1801 that ended in the sentencing to death of 39 prisoners. According to legend, the governor was loath to carry out so many executions, but to save face, he ordered that one body be strung up over and over again.

Southwest

Heading towards the airport, you pass several excellent sandy beaches, often with hardly anyone in sight. This is an inviting place to snorkel and go swimming in the surf. For a nominal admission, you can enjoy the spectacular stretch of fine sand at **Pigeon Point**, near the swampy Bon Accord Lagoon, whose shores attract many kinds of birds. There are changing rooms and cabanas, as well as a restaurant and bar.

Surfers head for **Mount Irvine Bay**, where you can play tennis on the courts of the hotel. The local Golf Club has an 18-hole championship course.

Buccoo Reef
The extensive coral reef lies offshore from Pigeon Point and Bon Accord Lagoon. Glass-bottom boats reveal the wonders of the warm tropical sea, and you'll marvel at the queen trigger-fish, blue tang, yellowtail, snapper and other beauties of the deep. For a clear view underwater, be sure to make the trip on a fair day at low tide. Good swimmers can use the snorkel equipment provided on the boats. The **Nylon Pool** has exceptionally clear water.

Caribbean Coast
The Northside Road leads northwest of Scarborough, passing Fort William, a well-maintained red-brick building that serves as the official residence of the Trinidad-Tobago president. A little further along you'll see a plantation Great House called The Whim.

Plymouth
A tombstone in Plymouth was inscribed in 1783 with an intriguing epitaph in memory of Betty Stiven: "A mother without knowing it, and a wife, without letting her husband know, except by her kind indulgences to him". Islanders translate this as a classic love affair between a master and his black mistress. She was the mother of the man's children, and was honoured by marriage to him only after her death, when the master finally recognized the children.

The **Great Courland Bay Monument**, situated on a headland, commands a striking view of the sea, and there is good swimming from the beach below. The monument was erected in memory of "the enterprising and industrious Courlanders from faraway Batavia on the Baltic shores, who lived in this area…" The cannon nearby mark the site of Fort James, built in 1768.

Arnos Vale
Continuing northeast along the coast you will see the Arnos Vale Hotel, built on a former sugar plantation. A disused sugar mill fitted out with a formidable crushing wheel made in Glasgow in 1857 stands in the grounds. If you book ahead, or join an organized tour, you can come here for the great event of the day: birdwatching at tea-time. As guests sit and sip their tea on the veranda, birds in all the colours of the rainbow flock down to feed: the yellow-breasted bananaquit, Tobago blue tanager, ruby topaz hummingbird and the handsome orange-breasted mot-mot or king of the woods.

Further along the Arnos Vale Road lies the **Adventure Farm and Nature Reserve**, a 5-ha (12-acre) tropical estate where you can watch birds and butterflies and pick your own luscious fresh fruit.

Beaches and Hikes

From Arnos Vale poor roads travel along the coast as far as Charlotteville. Scenic highlights include precipitous views of headlands and the sea, alternating with picturesque huts on stilts serving as bars, stores or post offices. There are good swimming beaches at **Castara Bay, Eng-lishman's Bay** and **Parlatuvier**, a fishing village with pastel houses. Rather than going all the way to Charlotteville, you can cross through the mountainous interior and the Tobago Forest Reserve (offering several hiking trails in the rainforest) to Roxborough, the second-largest town on the island, over on the Atlantic coast.

Atlantic Coast

The scenic Windward Road travels east from Scarborough, following the wild Atlantic coast. Tiny villages such as **Mesopotamia** and **Goldsborough** line the way. You may want to stop for a swim

at one of the bays just before Roxborough: Prince's, Queen's or King's. The **King's Bay Falls** are the highest on the island, and you can swim in the pools. With some time in hand, you could also hike to the three-tiered **Argyle Waterfall**, where guides will help you climb up the side.

Continue to **Speyside**, a colourful beach settlement. From here you can see the diving paradise of tiny **Goat Island** and **Little Tobago**, a 182-ha (450-acre) bird sanctuary, also called Bird-of-Paradise Island. In addition to the native birds that congregate here, there are dozens of other species, including gilt-plumed birds-of-paradise. The island supports dry forest and is an important breeding site for seabirds such as Audubon's shearwater, the brown booby and various terns.

The Windward Road then crosses the lush vegetation of the tip of the island to **Charlotteville**, a fishing village nestling beneath hills around Man o' War Bay. You can hike through the forest to **Pirate's Bay**, a favourite cove for swimming. No one has yet discovered the treasure said to be buried there.

A golden peach of a beach at Parlatuvier Bay. | **Larger than life and twice as exotic, feathered friends to take home with you.**

THE HARD FACTS

Airports. *Anguilla*: Wallblake Airport (AXA) in The Valley. *Antigua*: VC Bird International (ANU), 8 km (5 miles) northeast of St John's. *Barbados*: Grantley Adams International (BGI), 13 km (8 miles) east of Bridgetown. *Dominica*: Melville Hall (DOM), 64 km (40 miles) northeast of Roseau; Canefield (DCF) 5 km (3 miles) north of Roseau. *Grenada*: Maurice Bishop International (GND), 8 km (5 miles) south of St George's. *St Kitts*: Robert L. Bradshaw (SKB), 2 km (1 mile) from Basseterre. *Nevis*: Vance W. Amory International (NEV), 11 km (7 miles) from Charlestown. *St Lucia*: George F.L. Charles (SLU), 3 km (2 miles) from Castries; Hewanorra (UVF), 67 km (42 miles) from Castries. *St Vincent and the Grenadines*: ET Joshua (SVD), 3 km (2 miles) from Kingstown. There are small airports for light aircraft on Bequia, Union Island, Canouan and Mustique. *Trinidad*: Piarco International (POS), 27 km (17 mile) east of Port of Spain. *Tobago*: Crown Point (TAB), 13 km (8 miles) from Scarborough.

Banks. On most islands, open Monday to Thursday 8 a.m.–3 p.m.; Friday 8 a.m.–5 p.m.; some branches open on Saturday mornings, too. Grenada's banks close earlier (1.30 or 2 p.m.). Montserrat: Monday to Thursday 9 a.m.–2 p.m.; Friday 9 a.m.–3 p.m. Trinidad and Tobago Monday to Thursday 9 a.m.–4.30 p.m.; Friday 9–noon and 3–5 p.m.

Climate There is little variation in the temperature throughout the year. You can count on averages of 33– 35°C (91–95°F) during the day, with nights seldom cooler than 18°C (64°F). The trade winds temper the heat in coastal regions. From November to April, rainfall is at its lowest, though at all times showers exhaust themselves fairly quickly. Hurricanes can occur between June and November. Water temperature averages 29°C (84°F) and never falls below 25°C (77°F).

Clothing. For these tropical climes, lightweight, loose clothing is essential, preferably in comfortable cotton. Casual styles are the rule, unless you plan to stay in a luxury hotel, when women will want to dress up for formal evenings and men may require a jacket and possibly a tie. Above all, you'll need swimwear and a sunhat. It's advisable to bring along a long-sleeved jacket or cardigan for air-conditioned interiors or cooler evenings. A comfortable pair of sturdy, low-heeled walking shoes is indispensable for excursions.

Communications. The islands are linked to the US network. Country codes: Anguilla 1 264; Antigua 1 268; Barbados 1 246; Dominica 1 767; Grenada 1 473; Monserrat 1 664; St Kitts and Nevis 1 869, St Lucia 1 758, St Vincent and the Grenadines 1 784, Trinidad and Tobago 1 868. The international dialling code from all the islands is 011. Internet connection is available at major hotels; you'll find Internet cafés in the main towns.

Customs Allowance. There are slight variations from island to island but as a general rule travellers aged 18 years and over will be permitted 200 cigarettes or 50 cigars or 225 g tobacco; 1 litre wine or spirits.

Driving. Traffic drives on the left. Renting a car is the most flexible way to get round the islands. For the smaller isles, another option is to rent a motorcycle or scooter. In either case, the rental agency may require you to buy a visitor driver's licence. Island roads are often narrow and winding so drive carefully and respect the speed limits.

Language. English is the official language on all the islands; various Creole patois are also spoken.

Electricity. Barbados 110 volts AC, 50 Hz; Anguilla, Antigua, Montserrat, Trinidad and Tobago 110/220 volts AC, 60 Hz; St Lucia 220 volts AC, 50 Hz, St Kitts and Nevis 220 volts AC, 60 Hz; Dominica, Grenada, St Vincent and the Grenadines 220/240 volts AC, 50 Hz.

Holidays. Apart from New Year's Day, Good Friday, Easter Monday, Labour Day (May), Whit Monday, Christmas Day (and sometimes Boxing Day), common to all the islands, the following holidays are celebrated.
  Anguilla: May 30, Anguilla Day; June, Queen's Birthday; August 8, Constitution Day; December 19, Separation Day.
  Antigua: May, Bank Holiday; July, Caricom Day; August, Carnival Monday and Tuesday; November 1, Independence Day, December 9, National Heroes' Day.
  Barbados: January 21, Errol Barrow Day; April 28, National Heroes' Day; August 1, Emancipation Day; August, Kadooment Day; November 30, Independence Day.
  Dominica: February/March, Carnival; 1st Monday in August; November 3, Independence Day; November 4, Community Service Day.
  Grenada: February, Independence Day; May/June, Corpus Christi; August, Emancipation Day, Carnival; October 25, Thanksgiving.

Montserrat: March 17, St Patrick's Day; June, Queen's Birthday; July 18, Anniversary of Soufrière Hills Volcano Eruption; 1st Monday in August; December 31, Festival Day.

St Kitts and Nevis: December–January, Carnival; August, Emancipation Day; September 16, Heroes' Day; September 19, Independence Day.

St Lucia: January 2; February 22, Independence Day; May/June, Corpus Christi; August 1, Emancipation Day; October, Thanksgiving Day; December 13, National Day.

St Vincent and the Grenadines: March 14, National Heroes' Day; July, Carnival Monday and Tuesday; August, Emancipation Day; October 27, Independence Day.

Trinidad andTobago: March 30, Spiritual Baptist Shouters' Liberation Day; May 30, Arrival Day; May/June, Corpus Christi; June 19, Labour Day; August 1, Emancipation Day; August 31 Independence Day; September 24, Republic Day. Moveable: Eid ul Fitr (Muslim), Divali (Hindu).

Money. The East Caribbean dollar (EC$ or XCD), divided into 100 cents, is used on most of the islands. Coins from 1 ¢ to EC$1; banknotes from EC$5 to EC$100. US dollars can also be used. Exceptions are Barbados, Trinidad and Tobago. The Barbados dollar ($ or BBD) is issued in coins from 1¢ to $1; banknotes from $2 to $100. The Trinidad-Tobago dollar (TT$ or TTD) is issued in coins from 1 to 50 ¢; banknotes from TT$1 to TT$100. Keep your receipts to reconvert unspent Trinidadian money before you leave the islands. Major credit cards are widely accepted.

Post Office. Main post offices open Monday to Friday 8 or 8.30 a.m.– 3.30 p.m. or later, up to 5 p.m. In St Kitts and Nevis, St Lucia, St Vincent and the Grenadines, they also open Saturday mornings.

Time. GMT–4.

Tipping. If a service charge has not been added to the bill in restaurants and hotels, you may like to tip 10–15%.

Transport. For most places the best way to get around is by taxi. They generally have fixed rates between airport and hotels. Some islands have a minibus service with standard fares, or shared taxis on regular routes. Barbados has a frequent, cheap and comprehensive bus service.

Water. Bottled mineral water is advised, except on Barbados which has excellent spring water on tap.

An iconic fofoti (mangrove) tree on Eagle Beach in Aruba.

istockphoto.com/Tran

ARUBA, BONAIRE, CURAÇAO, SABA, SINT EUSTATIUS

The former island colonies of the Netherlands comprise two groups: the three S's, Saba, Sint Eustatius and Sint Maarten to the northeast among the Lesser Antilles, and the ABC islands Aruba, Bonaire and Curaçao, just north of the Venezuelan coast. In 1954 they gained autonomy as the Netherlands Antilles, to be officially dissolved on October 10, 2010.

Aruba

There are many reasons for visiting the honeymoon capital of the Caribbean. You'll find water sports galore, shopping bargains from all over the world, attractive scenery, spicy Indonesian food, friendly people—and glorious white sand beaches. Snorkelling and scuba fans appreciate Aruba's warm, clear waters teeming with vivid tropical fish. There are spectacular coral formations and even a few sunken vessels to be seen. You may want to try out a typically Aruban pastime: cart-sailing.

The island is only 32 km (20 miles) long by 10 km (6 miles) wide. From the capital, Oranjestad, there's a well-maintained coastal road and a network of secondary roads through the interior.

Oranjestad

The island's lovely old Dutch-gabled capital is situated on the southwestern coast. Walk along the wharf to the old schooner harbour. A lively open-air market takes place here every morning, as merchant-sailors sell fresh fish, fruit and vegetables directly off their boats to passers-by.

Wilhelminastraat

The street is a veritable showcase for the 18th-century houses of old Oranjestad—tall, narrow-gabled buildings with red-tiled roofs, painted in cool pastel shades, as well as intense yellows and royal blues, stuccoed with white decoration. This appealing chocolate-box architectural style can be seen throughout all the islands that formed the Netherlands Antilles.

ARUBA FLASHBACK

15th–16th centuries
Alonso de Ojeda discovers Aruba in 1499, claiming it for Spain, but the Spanish make little effort to exploit the island.

17th–18th centuries
The Dutch take over Aruba with little opposition from the Spanish in 1636. Peter Stuyvesant is appointed governor of Aruba and the other Dutch West Indian islands from 1643 to 1647, but spends most of these years on Curaçao and St Maarten

19th century–present
The British occupy Aruba in 1805, finally returning it to the Dutch in 1816. Gold is discovered on the island in 1824, and more than 1,350,000 kg of it is taken from the mines until around 1915, when declining yields force them to close.

In 1929, a large oil refinery opens on the island, bringing renewed prosperity. Aruba and five other Dutch-speaking islands form the autonomous federation of the Netherlands Antilles in 1954. Aruba secedes from the federation in 1986 and remains an autonomous part of the kingdom of the Netherlands. Offshore banking and oil refining are big business on Aruba, but tourism has taken over as the first industry: the island is very popular with American honeymooners. The population numbers 114,000.

Huber/Bertsch.

Fort Zoutman

The fort was built in 1796 and a lighthouse, the Willem III Tower, was added in 1870. It now houses a historical museum and hosts the Tuesday evening Bonbini festival (local crafts, food and music).

Shopping District

A vast number of shops cluster around **Caya G.F. Betico Croes** (former Nassaustraat). Since there's no sales tax in Aruba, you can find some real bargains in luxury articles from Latin America and Asia as well as Europe.

Seaport Village Mall

A five-minute walk from the harbour, this is Aruba's largest shopping centre with dozens of boutiques, restaurants and a casino.

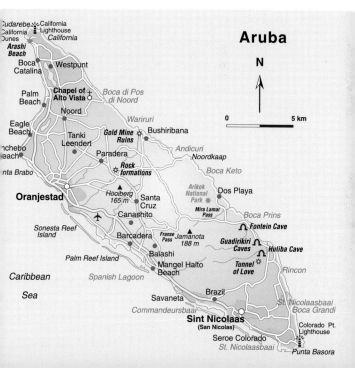

Sonesta Reef Island
You can take a boat to this private island a few hundred metres off the coast, have lunch at the hotel and visit the very secluded **Honeymoon Cove**, perfect for a romantic tête-à-tête.

West Coast
Begin sightseeing with a leisurely drive up the west coast, passing the fine white sands of Eagle Beach, then Palm Beach, lined with many of the island's luxury hotels.

De Olde Molen, a windmill built in Holland in 1804, was shipped across the Atlantic and reconstructed here in 1960. It has now been converted into a restaurant, offering a marvellous panorama from the terrace.

Just opposite the windmill is the **Bubali Bird Sanctuary**, where you can watch the antics of cormorants, herons, fish eagle and brown pelicans to your heart's content. More than 80 different migratory species flock to the area—don't forget to take your binoculars!

California Dunes
At the northwestern tip of Aruba, take a walk around California Dunes, the windy and barren site of an old lighthouse. Off the coast, the wreck of a World War II German freighter attracts scuba divers.

Noord
Heading back to the capital, take the road that leads inland to Noord and **St Ann's Church**, where you can see a lovely hand-carved oak altar, the work of a 19th-century Dutch artisan.

If you have time, make a detour to the tiny **Alto Vista chapel**, with stone pews outside. It dates only from 1952 but stands on the site of an earlier chapel put up by the Spanish.

From Noord, the road travels back to Oranjestad through the *cunucu*, as the countryside is called in Papiamento, dotted with brightly coloured houses, patches of cacti, enormous boulders, road signs featuring injunctions from the Lord's Prayer, and the emblematic *divi divi* trees, bent double by the trade winds.

Island Sights
Some of Aruba's most popular sights lie inland, within easy reach of Oranjestad.

Rock Gardens
At **Casibari** and the nearby **Hooiberg** ("Haystack Mountain"), you can see "rock gardens"—huge boulders weighing thousands of tons scattered near and far, as if thrown about by some crazed giant. Several of the boulders are engraved with ritual Indian carvings, centuries old, made by the the early inhabitants, Caribs or

Arawaks. The Hooiberg is not Aruba's tallest peak, but it features a long flight of steps that takes you 165 m (541 ft) to the top—a breathtaking look-out.

There are more rock gardens at **Ayo**, and from here you can continue to the north coast and the ghost town of **Bushiribana** with its abandoned goldmine. Long before gold-rush days, Bushiribana was a pirate's stronghold, and you'll spot the ruins of a pirate's castle that probably dates from the 16th century.

A coast road travels east from here to **Andicuri**, where over the centuries the pounding surf has carved a natural bridge out of the coral rock. An old coconut plantation on the inlet makes a particularly scenic spot for a picnic.

Caves

Not far from the town of Santa Cruz lie the caves of **Canashito**. Here you will see some mysterious hieroglyphs dating from the 12th to 15th centuries, made by Carib or Arawak Indians.

East of Santa Cruz, **Mira Lamar** nestles between Aruba's two highest peaks, Arikok, 176 m (577 ft), and Jamanota, 188 m (617 ft). The road rises to give some excellent views. Various caves in the area, all part of **Arikok National Park**, are decorated with Indian drawings, thought to have figured in ancient sacrificial rites.

Near **Guadirikiri Caves**, honeymooners may be intrigued by signs pointing out the **Tunnel of Love**. This is no romantic theme-park attraction, but in fact a large cave with a heart-shaped entrance, coloured walls and a resident bat colony.

East at **Dos Playa** and **Boca Prins**, you'll have a once-in-a-lifetime chance to try the unusual Aruban sport of dune-sliding. It's not at all difficult if you wear tennis shoes. At nearby **Fontein**, caves are decorated with Indian drawings, which, like the others on the island. may have been used as part of ancient sacrificial rites.

Balashi

The ghost town of Balashi was the centre of a profitable gold mining area in the 19th century. You can visit the abandoned mine and the ruins of a gold-smeltery.

Continue to **Frenchman's Pass** in the Aruba uplands, the haunt of the huge green parakeet, a species that can be found exclusively in this part of the Caribbean.

San Nicolas (Sint Nicolaas)

Back on the coast road, you can continue to San Nicolas, at the southeast tip of the island and its second-largest city. This modern community was built for the workers of Aruba's giant Lago Oil Refinery. East is the **Seroe Colorado** area, famous for its beaches.

Bonaire

Bonaire boasts some of the loveliest fringing reefs in the Caribbean—and more flamingos than people. Because of the abundant coral growth and variety of fish, the Netherlands Antilles National Parks Foundation has established a programme for reef protection. The whole island, surrounded by crystal-clear waters, forms a natural sanctuary, officially protected as the Bonaire Marine Park, where spear-fishing is strictly forbidden. Experts rate it one of the world's top spots for snorkelling and scuba-diving. Collection of black coral or other corals is allowed only for the Handicrafts Foundation. Forty diving spots have been designated and mooring buoys placed to prevent anchor damage to the reefs.

The island curves round with its back to the trade winds, sheltering the tiny capital of Kralendijk in the central crook of its western curve. Across the natural harbour lies the uninhabited rocky islet of Little Bonaire, a favourite picnic and diving spot.

Bonaire, 40 km (24 miles) long, is the driest island in the Caribbean, strewn with cactus and prickly pear. The south is sandy and flat, running down to salt pans, while the north is covered with rocky acacia-clad hills, culminating in 241-m (784-ft) Mount Brandaris. Iguanas and goats thrive here, and vivid green parakeets that dig nests deep into termite mounds.

Kralendijk

The name means "coral dike", and it is easy to see why: the beaches that sweep away to north and south are edged by coral reefs running out 90 m (100 yd) into the blue-green sea. The town's population of 3000 live in trim colour-washed houses set in neat gardens.

By the harbour, the **fish market** is housed in a miniature Greek temple. Nearby, **Fort Oranje** displays a 150-year-old cannon. The museum, Sabana 14, is worth a visit to see artefacts from Bonaire homes and to learn something of the island's early history.

Island Sights

Those who want to snorkel or scuba-dive will head straight to Lac Bay or one of the diving spots along the reefs, and there's no lack of choice for beaches, *playas* and *bokas* for those who prefer swimming and sailing. If you prefer to stay dry, take a day trip right round the island and a tour of the reefs in a glass-bottomed boat.

Washington Slagbaai National Park

Inland from the storage depot, where supertankers unload oil,

Gotomeer is a blue salt lake edged by brilliant roseate flamingos feeding long-legged in the shallows. Occasionally great flights of the birds take off, unravelling like a piece of pink knitting and circling round to land again and resume their feast of algae.

The lake lies on the edge of the national park, a 5,450-ha reserve with **Mount Brandaris** as its centre point. A road runs through the park's rugged wilderness where a rich variety of birds (130 species have been counted) can be observed, including parrots, parakeets and humming birds.

Rincón
The village was once the home of black slaves who worked in the salt pans. From here you can visit **Boca Onima** on the northeast coast to view shallow caves with rock carvings coloured in red, the work of the original Indian inhabitants and estimated to be more than 500 years old. Archaeologists have so far failed to decipher them.

Lac Bay
An arc of mangroves curves round the lagoon at Lac Bay, where the fishermen harvest conch and leave the shells piled up on the beach. This is the ideal spot for a swim in safe, clear water—or a trip in a glass-bottomed boat. Seas wash in and out

Huber/Gräfenhain

Flamingos at lunch in the salt flats of Pekelmeer.

over a coral reef into a bay, making it the perfect nursery for fish and a favourite diving spot.

Flamingo Sanctuary
On **Pekelmeer**, on the southern tip of the island, you'll find the largest colony of flamingos in the western hemisphere, numbering over 10,000. In spring, the birds build their round mud nests and raise their young on the salt flats where the local salt company has set aside a reserve of 125 acres (50 ha). Watch them sieving water through their hooked beaks

BONAIRE FLASHBACK

Early times
Bonaire is settled by Caiquetio Indians, an Arawak tribe from South America, who carve inscriptions in the island caves.

15th–16th centuries
A Spanish landing party from Amerigo Vespucci's expedition discovers the island in 1499. The Indians are deported to Hispaniola to work in the copper mines.

17th–18th centuries
The Dutch succeed the Spanish in 1623 and start producing salt, using imported slaves. Spanish and English pirates call regularly at the island to requisition food.

19th century
The British take over and leave the island with 300 slaves to a US planter. The Dutch return in 1815. With the abolition of slavery in 1863, the salt trade becomes uneconomic and is abandoned.

20th century–present
The salt trade is revived. North of Kralendijk, a storage depot is built for transshipment of oil from Africa and the Middle East destined for the United States. Tourism expands, and Flamingo Airport is built south of Kralendijk. The population numbers 14,000. In 2008, the Netherlands Antilles break up and Bonaire becomes a special municipality of the Netherlands itself.

istockphoto.com/Hofmeester

to feed on the brine shrimps and algae which give them their startling pink colour.

The **Willemstoren Lighthouse**, built in 1837, rises on the coast just before you reach the main salt pans ringed by pyramids of white salt. The salt is deposited by the sea in ponds and dried into crystals by sun and wind.

Three tall stone obelisks on the shore in the Dutch colours of red, white and blue once guided ships to their moorings by the ponds. Along the beach, the remains of 19th-century **slave huts** have been restored. The slaves worked here all week and at weekends trekked 24 km (15 miles) across the island to their homes in Rincón.

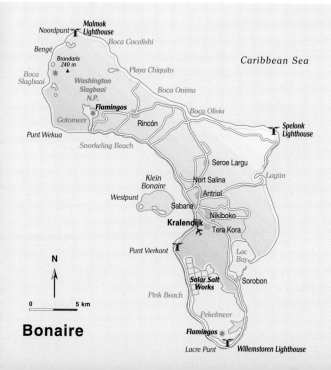

Caribbean Sea

Bonaire

Curaçao

A fragment of Amsterdam set adrift in the West Indies, Willemstad is the most European of Caribbean cities. Curaçaoans seem particularly adept at reconciling old-world charm with the business-like present. Lovely 18th-century Dutch colonial houses look out over St Anna Bay, while cruise ships and giant oil tankers glide by on their way to one of the world's busiest ports. Business is booming, but landmarks are carefully preserved.

The island, 60 km (38 miles) long and 12 km (7 miles) wide, has a population of about 192,000, made up of scores of different nationalities. If you venture out into the countryside, you will find a few scattered windmills, some old Dutch plantation houses and a good deal of arid, windy land with cactus and divi-divi trees.

Willemstad

The old center of Willemstad is a UNESCO World Heritage site. Right through the middle of Willemstad runs St Anna Bay (really an inlet connecting the Caribbean with the Schottegat deep-water port). On the east side is the **Punda**, the city's oldest district, on the west, the **Otrabanda** ("the other side"). Edged with

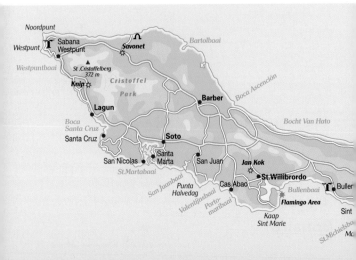

fine Dutch colonial houses, the bustling bay provides the best show in town. A never-ending procession of small sailing boats, sleek cruise ships and lumbering oil tankers parades back and forth between Schottegat and the Caribbean Sea, with spectators nearly always around to watch the ships.

Queen Emma Bridge

This floating pontoon bridge, which swings open on a hinge to let the ships by, was the ingenious idea of an enterprising American, Leonard B. Smith, the same man who brought ice and electricity to Curaçao. At first,

back in 1888, they charged a toll: 2¢ for those wearing shoes but free for the barefooted, the laudable intention being to tax only those with the means to pay. But, it seems, the poor often borrowed or bought sandals so they could pay, while the well-heeled (financially speaking) liked to take off their shoes and cross for nothing. The authorities eventually gave up and now everyone goes over free, shoes or not.

For many years, the Queen Emma was the bay's only bridge, and every time it opened for ships the road traffic backed up for miles. In 1974, an arching, four-lane bridge was inaugurated

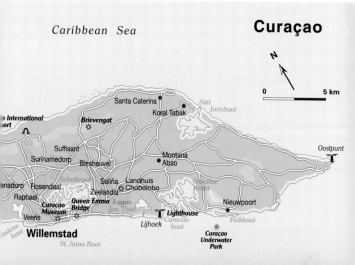

CURAÇAO FLASHBACK

15th–16th centuries
Curaçao is discovered in 1499 by Alonso de Ojeda, one of Columbus' lieutenants. Also part of the expedition is Amerigo Vespucci, who goes ashore, meets the towering Caiquetio Indians and pronounces Curaçao the "island of giants." Led by Juan de Ampues, the Spanish settle Curaçao in 1527 but they never make very much of it.

17th–18th centuries
The Netherlands West India Company takes the island in 1634, chasing the Spaniards off to Latin America. Curaçao becomes the main Dutch trading base in the region. Peter Stuyvesant is sent to the upcoming island as governor in 1642. The city of Willemstad grows up around Fort Amsterdam, as the Dutch build neat houses on carefully laid out streets resembling the ones they left behind. They also erect a series of forts. Jews from Spain and Portugal, fleeing the Inquisition, arrive in the 1650s to seek their fortunes in the tolerant Dutch colony. Willemstad flourishes as a trading centre—especially for slave-trading.

19th century
The British establish in 1800 a "protectorate" over Curaçao and take the island, briefly, during the Napoleonic Wars. Treaty of London in 1816 restores Curaçao to Dutch hands. Slavery is abolished in 1863 and the island's economy goes into decline.

20th century–present
The Royal Dutch Shell Company selects Curaçao as the site for a refinery to process Venezuelan oil. The petroleum industry brings prosperity to Curaçao; the people who come from all parts of the globe to work here bring a cosmopolitan tone. When Curaçao and five other islands win autonomy from the Netherlands in 1954 to form the Netherlands Antilles, Willemstad is chosen as its capital. In 2008, the Netherlands Antilles break up, and Curaçao is granted autonomy within the Kingdom of the Netherlands (status aparte).

for vehicular traffic. With its 56-m (185-ft) high span, the Queen Juliana Bridge allows all but the tallest ships to sail right under it.

St Anna Bay

The buildings along St Anna Bay house elegant shops and restaurants. The Dutch imprint here is unmistakable — narrow, gabled, three- and four-storey structures with red-tiled roofs. The tiles were brought over the ocean as ballast on ships; for the return trip the vessels were filled with salt that the Dutch used to cure herring. As for the rainbow colours of the 18th-century houses — the cool pastels, the vibrant yellows and blues — we have an early governor of Curaçao to thank. The poor man suffered from ferocious headaches, and the glare of the tropical sun on the white buildings hurt his eyes. So he ordered that every house be painted any colour but white.

Two forts guarded the entrance to St Anna Bay. On the east side, the **Waterfort** was built in 1634. A hotel now welcomes guests within its walls but the cannons remain.

Near the pontoon bridge on the Punda side, the lovely golden yellow **Penha Building**, with white trim, is one of the city's oldest houses (1708). It sits at the corner of the two main shopping streets, Breedestraat and Heerenstraat.

Fort Amsterdam

Imposing mustard walls surround Fort Amsterdam, the historic centre of Willemstad. Construction probably began before 1642, when Governor Peter Stuyvesant was in residence. Now it's the seat of government. The complex of buildings consists of various offices, the **Governor's Residence** — a gracious Dutch colonial mansion with 19th-century additions — and the **Fort Church**, which has a British cannonball lodged in one of its walls, and is worth seeing for its lovely stained-glass windows.

Mikve Israel-Emanuel Synagogue

Dating from 1732, the Dutch colonial synagogue, right in the middle of the shopping district, is the oldest in the Western Hemisphere. Its congregation was founded some 80 years earlier by a dozen families of Sephardic Jews who came to Curaçao from Amsterdam. Bright yellow outside, richly furnished within, the synagogue has four magnificent bronze chandeliers, replicas of the ones in Amsterdam's Portuguese Synagogue. But perhaps the most striking feature is the floor — a carpet of white sand, symbolizing the desert where the

Bernard Joliat

Travelling inland, you'll discover many fine plantation houses open to the public.

Jews wandered in their search for the Promised Land.

The **Synagogue Museum** was once a rabbi's home and later a Chinese laundry. But the discovery of a 300-year-old mikvah, or ritual bath, in the courtyard led to extensive restoration of the 18th-century house. The museum contains many valuable historical objects linked with Jewish ritual.

Postal Museum

The museum is housed in a bright red building with a pointed gable, dating from 1693 and restored in 1990. At the corner of Kuiperstraat and former Keukenstraat, it is the oldest townhouse in Willemstad.

Floating Market

Try to visit the market in the morning, when it's most lively. Small boats from Venezuela bring fresh produce and fish, returning home after they have sold their merchandise. Haggling is still the order of the day — whether you're buying a piece of fabric or some exotic fruit.

Scharloo

The Wilhelmina drawbridge leads to Scharloo, where wealthy Jewish merchants used to live. You'll see some of the finest homes in Willemstad here, ranging from early colonial to Victorian.

On the hill behind Scharloo, **Roosevelt House** has a black-tiled roof and American flag. It was a gift from the people of Curaçao to the US in appreciation for assistance during World War II. The US Consul General has his office and residence there.

Curaçao Museum

In the Otrabanda District, a Dutch plantation house which served in its time as a seaman's hospital has now been refurbished as the Curaçao Museum, boasting an interesting collection of colonial furnishings and relics of the Caiquietio Indian culture.

Fort Nassau

You will find the very best view of Willemstad at Fort Nassau, 60 m (200 ft) above the inner harbour. From the fort or its restaurant you can look down on the toy city below. You can also see the gigantic oil refinery, reduced to lilliputian dimensions by the distance.

Seaquarium

One of Willemstad's star attractions is the Seaquarium complex, stretching along the largest beach on Curaçao. You can enjoy a fascinating collection of sea-life and take a trip in a glass-bottom boat. There are also water sports and a variety of shops and restaurants.

Island Sights

As you travel around the island, you'll see some fine old Dutch plantation houses, or *landhuizen*.

Brievengat

The 18th-century estate restored by the government after hurricane desolation and general dilapidation, is now open for visits; they stage folklore shows.

Chobolobo

Curaçao liqueur is made at Chobolobo, in Salinja. The fragrant peel of a green citrus *(laraha)* that grows only on this island gives the liqueur its distinctive flavour; the fruit is like a very bitter orange, considered inedible. Tours of the Senior Liqueur Distillery premises are followed by a tasting session. While you're there, admire the architecture of the 17th-century *landhuis*.

Jan Kok Landhuis

This mansion dates from the 18th century. If you time your visit right you might get to taste some Dutch pancakes while absorbing the view of the flamingos stepping daintily along the salt flats.

Savonet

The 17th-century *landhuis* is privately owned, but there's a small museum nearby. This is the signal that you've arrived at **Christoffel Park**, a spacious preserve criss-crossed by marked walking trails. You can climb Mount Christoffel, 375 m (1,230 ft) or stay closer to sea level and observe the birds and deer, and the stands of cactus and aloe.

Hato Caves

In these caves overlooking the airport, the stalactites and stalagmites are given the star treatment through lighting effects. Take one of the guided tours on Sundays; not a lot of exertion is involved.

Benelux Press

Saba and Sint Eustatius (Statia)

Twin dots in the ocean, near the top of the great sweep of the Eastern Caribbean islands, Saba and Statia are largely ignored by the tourism business. No beaches to speak of, hardly any roads, no noise and bustle—their sunny charm lies in their very simplicity and friendliness. These are not identical twins. While Saba is mountainous and rugged, its coast dropping sheer into the sea, Statia is green and lush, and it has a few beaches. But one thing they both have in common is their idyllic, carefree lifestyle.

Saba, the tip of an extinct volcano, 45 km (28 miles) south of Sint Maarten, is the smallest of all the Dutch islands, covering a mere 13 sq km (5 sq miles). Next in size at 21 sq km (8 sq miles) comes Statia, 27 km (17 miles) to the southeast of Saba. Though the islands are special Dutch municipalities, most of the place names, surnames and conversations are in English.

By Caribbean standards, Saba (1,000 inhabitants) and Statia (2,000) are poor islands, the tradi-

istockphoto.com/Li

Nestling in a valley, The Bottom, Saba's red-roofed capital. | Saba is formed from an extinct volcano and is a top scuba diving destination.

tional economic activities of agriculture, fishing and trading now being supplemented by low-key tourism. It's a far cry from its 18th-century heyday, when thousands of settlers and slaves milled around and the islands' riches were fought over by Spanish, French, English and Dutch.

Either island can easily be seen in a day. But many devotees come for longer, to enjoy the peace and quiet and scenery, ranging from rugged rock to tropical gardens ablaze with hibiscus, frangipani and oleanders, and from meadows and farmland to dark rainforest where man-sized ferns shade the mountain paths.

Saba

Its four villages—The Bottom, Windwardside, St John's and Hell's Gate—are strung out across the island, linked by a single road. Until the 1940s they could be reached only by steps hewn from the rock. When Dutch engineers were summoned to see about the possibility of building a road in the 1930s, they said it was impossible. Proving them wrong, a resourceful islander took a correspondence course in engineering and spent the next twenty years on his concrete thoroughfare, circumscribing the island's contours, up hill and down dale. The road even splits in two at one point, to avoid a tree.

There are no beaches on Saba, apart from a single stretch of dark volcanic sand at Well's Bay.

The Bottom

The name of the minuscule capital, The Bottom, is derived from the old Zeeland word for a bowl *(botte)* since it lies in a valley surrounded by hills. Among the few sights here are the Lieutenant-Governor's official residence, and the small garden park which adjoins it. Take a look, too, at **The Ladder**—524 steps cut into the rock—once the sole means of access for passengers and cargo arriving by sea.

Windwardside

Saba's second largest settlement, almost 1,000 ft (300 m) higher up, is an idyllic little village with red-roofed clapboard or white-washed houses and gardens fragrant with hibiscus and oleander. Attractions here include several tourist shops and two period-piece inns. The **Saba Museum** is housed in a sea captain's cottage around 150 years old, displaying interesting old family heirlooms, including a mahogany four-poster bed.

Peaks

On the outskirts of Windwardside are the 1,064 hand-hewn steps leading to the top of **Mount Scenery**, at 887 m (2,910 ft) Saba's

SABA AND STATIA FLASHBACK

16th–17th centuries

Saba is sighted by Sir Francis Drake in 1595 and by Dutchman Pieter Schouten in 1624 and his compatriot Piet Heyn two years later. In 1632 shipwrecked Englishmen land on uninhabited Saba, three years before France claims the island. The Dutch settle on Statia in 1636 and build Fort Oranje, then occupy Saba in the 1640s. The English, Dutch, French and Spanish dispute the islands.

18th century

Trade in sugar, tobacco and cotton brings slaves and prosperity to the islands, particularly Statia which is nicknamed "The Golden Rock". During the American War of Independence, Statia is an important trans-shipment centre for guns and other supplies to American troops. On November 16, 1776 she unknowingly fires the first salute to a ship flying the new American colours. In retaliation, in 1781, Admiral Rodney and his British soldiers ransack Fort Oranje. The following year the French arrive. The economy never recovers.

19th century

In 1816 both Saba and Statia finally become Dutch, Saba having changed hands 12 times and Statia 22 in the preceding two and a half centuries. The emancipation of plantation-working slaves in 1863 creates a labour shortage and hastens the decline of the islands, which sink to an existence dependent on subsistence from the sea and the few crops that can be grown in the poor volcanic soil.

20th century–present

Saba's one and only road is built in the 1930s and 40s. During World War II, Queen Wilhelmina promises the islands independence. A charter in 1954 gives domestic autonomy but proclaims the islands an integral part of the Kingdom of the Netherlands. Tourism helps to improve the economy after the construction of airports on both islands, but, almost beachless, they remain relatively uncommercialized. In 1989 Hurricane Hugo wreaks havoc with Statia's geography. Saba's new University of Medicine brings in more revenue. Since the break-up of the Netherlands Antilles in 2008, Saba and Statia remain in effect part of the Netherlands itself as special municipalities.

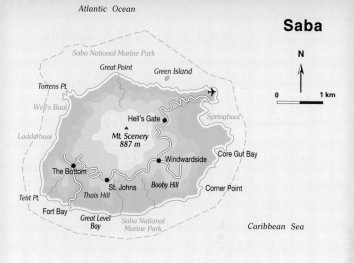

Saba

Atlantic Ocean

Saba National Marine Park

Great Point

Green Island

Torrens Pt.

N

0   1 km

Well's Baai

Hell's Gate

Springbaai

Ladderbaai

Mt. Scenery
887 m

Windwardside

Core Gut Bay

The Bottom

St. Johns

Booby Hill

Tent Pt.

Thais Hill

Corner Point

Fort Bay

Great Level
Bay

Saba National
Marine Park

Caribbean Sea

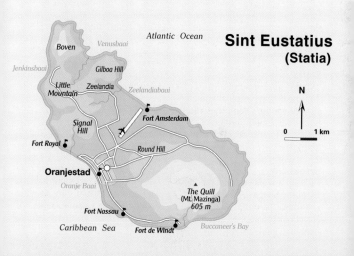

**Sint Eustatius
(Statia)**

Atlantic Ocean

Boven

Venusbaai

Jenkinsbaai

Gilboa Hill

Little
Mountain

Zeelandia

Zeelandiabaai

N

0   1 km

Signal
Hill

Fort Amsterdam

Fort Royal

Round Hill

Oranjestad

Oranje Baai

The Quill
(Mt. Mazinga)
605 m

Fort Nassau

Caribbean Sea

Fort de Windt

Buccaneer's Bay

highest point, often with its head in the clouds. Much less strenuous are the 60 steps to the top of **Bobby Hill Peak**, which from its 460 m (1,500 ft) also offers a panoramic view of the island and the other hiking trails thoughtfully laid out by the tourist authority.

Saba Marine Park

With good visibility down to a depth of 30 m (100 ft) or more, an increasing number of snorkellers and scuba-divers are being lured to a submarine wonderland of caverns and corals and reef fish of all kinds. Efforts made to preserve Saba's marvellous heritage resulted in the creation, in 1987, of the extensive Saba Marine Park. The tourist office or one of the diving centres can give information about lessons, equipment hire and trips.

Statia

"Statia" is a contraction of "St Anastasia", the original name bestowed on the island by Columbus. The Dutch preferred Sint Eustatius but the original abbreviation stuck.

Oranjestad

Pick up a walking tour brochure from the tourist office and enjoy strolling through the quaint streets of the capital, more a village than a city, filled with small,

Dutch-style houses. The chief monument is the ruined **Fort Oranje**, put up in 1636 to guard (unsuccessfully, as it turned out) against intruders. Complete with cannon, it's a great lookout post that will give you the feel of the island's history, as well as some excellent camera shots.

For more insight into the past, visit the 18th-century Doncker-de Graaff House, now the **Sint Eustatius Historical Foundation Museum**. The island's prosperous heyday is brought alive in exhibits and reconstructed rooms, and there's also a section on pre-Hispanic history, including the 1,500-year-old skeleton of an Arawak Indian.

Other sights worth a quick peek are the warehouses and taverns, some of which are undergoing restoration, and the 18th-century places of worship with their adjoining graveyards—**Honen Dalim Synagogue**, built in 1738, and the Dutch Reformed Church—all attesting to the rise and fall of the island's fortunes.

Hikes

The interior is sparsely populated, and large areas are untouched by human hand. If you're a nature lover, you'll find interesting hiking through the tropical forests. The tourist office can provide details of the various trails, for some of which you may need a guide.

A popular goal is the rather steep climb to The Quill, the extinct volcano that dominates the island's silhouette. Its rainforest crater is full of breadfruit trees, orchids and lianas, as well as land crabs that the locals catch to put in the pot. Good views can be had from its summit and from Gilboa Hill at the other end of the island. Here and there on your travels you might spot ruins of the old forts and batteries.

Beaches

It must be admitted that Statia's beaches do not live up to most people's idea of an idyllic palm-fringed strand. Oranje Beach, near the capital, is safe for swimming and watersports. Beaches on the windward, Atlantic side are sandy and scenic, but unsafe for swimming because of a strong undertow. The limpid waters round the island provide excellent diving and snorkelling, particularly for those interested in nosing around wrecks of the old trading ships that came to grief hereabouts. The tourist office and diving centres can supply details and equipment.

The 1781 headquarters of Admiral Rodney now house the Oranjestad museum. | Colourful sails catching the wind. | The Saban anole (Anolis sabanus), a lizard endemic to Saba.

Benelux Press

Fotolia.com/Sapsiwai

istockphoto.com/Valtenbergs

THE HARD FACTS

Airports. *Aruba*: Queen Beatrix (AUA), 3 km (2 miles) southeast of Oranjestad. *Bonaire*: Flamingo Airport (BON), 4 km (2.5 miles) from Kralendijk. *Curaçao*: Hato (CUR), 12 km (7 miles) from Willemstad. *Saba*: Juancho Yrausquin (SAB) at Cove Bay has one of the world's shortest runways (international travel is via Saint-Martin). *Statia*: FD Roosevelt (EUX) airstrip, near Oranjestad, is served by daily scheduled flights from St Kitts and Nevis, Saint-Martin and Saba.

Banks. Open Monday to Friday 8 or 8.30 a.m.–4 or 4.30 p.m. (1 p.m. in Statia, to 4 or 5 p.m. Fridays). Some close for lunch. Curaçao Monday to Friday 8 a.m.–3.30 p.m.

Climate. The islands have warm weather year-round, with average temperatures most often between 24° and 29° C (75° and 85° F). The hurricane season is from June to November.

Clothing. Lightweight clothes for daytime. A sweater may come in handy for cool evenings, especially at higher altitudes, and you might take something to protect your hair against the trade winds.

Communications. Country codes: Aruba 297; other islands 599. The international access code is oo. Large hotels have Internet access, and you will find Internet cafés in the main towns.

Customs Allowance. The following items may be imported by persons over 15 years of age without incurring customs duty: 200 cigarettes or 50 cigars or 250 g tobacco; 2 litres alcoholic beverages (Aruba 1 litre spirits or 2.25 l wine or 3 l beer).

Driving. Aruba and Curaçao have good roads. On Bonaire they are reasonable, and Saba has just one road winding diagonally across the island. On Statia, there is a road of sorts, and as many donkeys as cars. Drive on the right. The minimum age for renting a car is 21 or 26. For Curaçao an International Driving Permit is required; for the other islands a valid foreign licence held for at least two years is sufficient.

Electricity. Aruba 110 volts AC, 60 Hz; Bonaire 127 volts AC, 50 Hz; Curaçao, Saba, Statia 110/220 volts AC, 50 Hz.

Holidays. Apart from New Year, Easter, April 30 Queen's Birthday, May 1 Labour Day, Ascension Day and Christmas, which they have in common, the islands celebrate the following holidays. *Aruba*: January 25, GF Croes Day; February or March, Lenten Carnival; March 18, Aruba Flag Day. *Bonaire*: September 6, Bonaire Flag Day; October 21, Antilles Day. *Curaçao*: February or March, Carnival Monday; July 2, Curaçao Flag Day; October 21, Antilles Day. *Saba*: August, Carnival Monday; October 21, Antilles Day; 1st Monday in December, Saba Day. *Statia*: July 1, Emancipation Day; end July, Carnival Monday; October 21, Antilles Day; November 16, St Eustatius Day.

Language. The official language in the ABC islands is Dutch, and many people also speak English and Spanish. Papiamento, the local tongue, is a mixture of Dutch, Spanish, Portuguese and a sprinkling of English, French, Carib Indian and West African dialects. In Saba and Statia the official language is English but Dutch is also taught in school. Papiamento, French and Spanish are also spoken on Statia.

Money. The Aruban florin (AFl or AWG) is divided into 100 cents. Coins range from 5 cents to 5 AFl; banknotes from 10 to 500 AFl. On the other islands, the official currency is the Netherlands Antilles florin or guilder (NAf), divided into 100 cents. Coins range from 1 cent to 5 NAf, banknotes from 10 to 100 NAf. In many shops you can pay in US dollars. Major credit cards are widely accepted by most hotels, better restaurants and shops. Travellers cheques are also accepted. Because of the islands' change in status, the currency is liable to change in the future.

Shops. Open Monday to Saturday 8 or 9 a.m. to 6 or 6.30 p.m. Some close during lunch hours.

Time. GMT−4, all year round.

Tipping. Most restaurant bills include a service charge (15%). If not, a tip of 10–15% is normal. Hotels add a government tax of 5–10% plus a 10% service charge. Waiters and taxi drivers also expect a tip.

Transport. Depend on taxis for the short distances involved; rates are fixed. There are plenty of boats at the piers for scenic runs or diving, and a public bus service on the larger islands.

Water. Bottled mineral water is available everywhere.

The vendors will give you the low-down on their fruit and vegetables in Grenada's market.

Claude Thibault-Bazin

DINING OUT

The main ingredients in Caribbean cooking are colour and spice—and all things nice. The islands have drawn on the culinary traditions of Africa, Europe and America, modifying the result to suit the local produce. You'll come across unfamiliar vegetables and luscious fruit. And if new savours and flavours don't appeal, there are plenty of "international" gourmet restaurants, and you may even find your favourite fast-food outlet, too.

Soups

Creamy soups made from avocado, breadfruit or pumpkin are found all over the Caribbean. Highly spiced pigeon-pea soup is usually made with coconut milk and a little ham or salt-pork. More substantial, *kallaloo* or *calaou* is concocted from dasheen leaves (similar to spinach), okra, onions, garlic, crab, salt pork or beef, chicken stock, coconut milk and hot pepper seasoning to taste.

Starters

For something lighter than soup, try *pastelles* or *doucana*, plantain or banana leaves stuffed with a corn meal and savoury meat filling. In the Dutch islands they are called *ayacas*. *Accras*, fried codfish balls, are served with a piquant sauce or "floats"—puffy, fried yeast biscuits.

Seafood

Conch (or *lambi*), a shellfish that resembles oyster meat, turns up in stews and chowders and as a marinated cocktail. It can also be served with garlic and herbs, lemon and butter, lime sauce or spicier Creole sauces. Spiny lobster often appears as an appetizer, garnished with seaweed. Crab backs are shells stuffed with spicy crabmeat filling.

As for fish, ask for the catch of the day and you won't be disappointed. Local varieties include red snapper, kingfish, bonito, yellow-fin tuna and dolphin (not the porpoise). In the Virgin Islands, fish is properly served with Johnny Cake, absolutely delicious when served piping hot. Corrupted from "Journey Cake", the simple fried dough was prepared for men going out for a long day's work in the fields. Be sure to try flying fish, a speciality of Barbados: it's lightly fried and served with lime wedges and tartare sauce or cut into fingers and deep-fried. Codfish (or salt fish) and ackee is another favourite, sometimes offered as a breakfast dish. The rosy ackee fruit is poisonous until it ripens and bursts open, revealing a delicate yellow interior. When cooked, it tastes somewhat like scrambled eggs.

Meat
Generally you'll find good steaks and other cuts of beefs, as well as pork and lamb. There's also chicken and duck, and on some island, stewed goat. One outstanding meat dish is *pepperpot*, which originated with the South American Indians. It's a succulent stew of pork, beef and chicken, though the key ingredient is *casareep*, a spicy mixture of grated cassava, cinnamon and brown sugar.

Sancoche is similar, blending pork and pig's tail, beef, cassava, yams, potatoes, peppers, and perhaps a splash of coconut milk.

Vegetables
Your main meal may be accompanied by sweet potato, breadfruit, okra, cassava root, taro or fried plantain, a larger, coarser cousin of the banana. Rice is fre-

Salt Island spice. Many of the islands have their own seasoning to add spice to meat, fish, soups and stews. One of the tangiest comes from Salt Island in the BVI. Called Caribbean seasoning, it's a blend of Salt Island salt, thyme, chibble (chives), black peppercorns, whole cloves, hot yellow peppers, fresh celery, nutmeg, mace and garlic.

quently served with curry and coconut milk or with red beans (rice'n'peas). *Chocho* is a prickly fruit with a taste somewhat like marrow. Christophene is a kind of squash and can be delicately sautéed or served in a cream sauce.

Both *dasheen* (the tuberous part) and breadfruit may be boiled, sautéed or fried. *Coo-coo* technically means a side dish, but here usually implies corn meal or semolina cooked in a mould.

Local Flavour
Cayman specialities feature turtle meat, fresh from the green turtle farm. Try it in tasty soup or stew, or the truly memorable steaks.

In Jamaica, "stamp and go" are fried fishcakes, while Solomon Gundy is a well-seasoned pickled herring. Jerk pork—highly peppered pork that has been smoked over pimento wood—is a speciality of the Jamaican east coast. The recipe came from the runaway Maroons, who originally used it on wild boar.

Puerto Rico, naturally, has a Spanish flavour. On street stalls you'll find deep-fried codfish fritters *(bacalaítos fritos)*, deep-fried meat and cheese turnovers *(pastelillos)* and banana croquettes stuffed with beef or pork *(alcapurrias)*. *Tostones* are fried plantain slices, something like potato chips. Nothing is more typically Puerto Rican than *asopao*, a rice stew with chicken, seafood or pigeon peas. Visitors do not always share the local enthusiasm for this soupy creation, but there are lots of other nice rice dishes to choose from, such as the Spanish standbys *paella* and *arroz con pollo* or "simple" rice and beans. For your first course, Puerto Rican black bean soup *(sopa de habichuelas negras)* can be superb. It's best garnished with chopped onion.

On the Virgin Islands, treat yourself to *gundy*, a flavoursome pâté of salt cod or lobster mashed with olives, onions and peppers.

In the French West Indies, the same ingredients are used, but with names you'll find more difficult to decipher: *féroce d'avocat* is a spicy mixture of avocado and grilled cod, while *matoutou de crabes* is a dish of sautéed crab meat with onions, garlic, hot pepper, lemon juice, thyme and other seasonings. *Blaff* combines fresh fish with lime, garlic and hot red pepper, while *ti nin lan morue* presents cod with an escort of green bananas, sweet potatoes, peppers, cucumbers and pork.

One of Antigua's more unusual dishes is *souse*, boiled pig's head and trotters served with lime juice, sliced cucumber and pepper. *Doucanah* is a sweet potato dumpling flavoured with coconut and raisins, traditionally boiled in banana leaves. It is served with codfish, anchovies and eggplant.

Surprises await you on Dominica and Montserrat: "mountain chicken" actually refers to frog's legs (belonging to the giant land frog), and "goat water" is a tasty stew of goat simmered together with yams, breadfruit, pumpkin and cassava.

Street stands in Trinidad sell spicy Indian specialities such as deep-fried *kachouris* (chickpea fritters), *poulouris* (balls of split-pea flour), and *sahinas* (ground split-pea fritters with saffron). Use the accompanying sauces with caution. *Roti* stands provide pepper-hot curry stews wrapped in a *chapati*. *Pacro* is widely available at festival times: a shellfish stew that is reputed for its aphrodisiac powers.

Popular on the Dutch islands, *sopito* is a fish and coconut soup flavoured with salt pork and assorted spices. Among the more unusual main dishes, try *keshi yena*, Edam cheese stuffed with meat, chicken or fish and raisins, then baked; and *capucijners*, a combination of meat, bacon, onions and pickles. *Stoba*, a highly seasoned lamb or goat stew is often served with banana fritters. It may interest you to know that *soppi juana* is iguana soup and *zult* pickled pigs' ears.

Indonesia in the Caribbean. In the former Netherlands Antilles, don't miss the chance to sample authentic Indonesian *rijsttafel*, an array of 20 to 30 different fish and meat dishes served with rice. Among them: *ikan asem manis* (sweet-sour fish), *babi ketjap* (pork cooked in sweet soy sauce), *semur sapi* (beef stew with tomatoes) and so on. You'll get a small dish of *sambal* on the side—lime juice and hot chillies mixed to a paste with roasted shrimp or fish (approach with caution). *Nasi goreng* is fried rice with meat or shrimp and vegetables, seasoned with garlic and spices—*bami goreng* if the rice is replaced by noodles. *Saté* is also popular: beef, chicken, mutton or prawns are marinated in sugared spices, skewered and cooked over charcoal, accompanied by a peanut sauce.

Dessert

Sample some of the exotic local fruits: mango, papaya (paw paw), passionfruit, tamarind, coconut, pineapple, sweetsop and soursop and many others that never find their way to our supermarket shelves. You'll also find these fruits turned into tantalizing salads (with a dash of rum), pies, cakes and puddings—and juices, of course. Coconut tarts are especially delicious. Puerto Rico has an intriguing dessert: *dulce de lechosa con queso blanco*, papaya cubes cooked in sugar and cinnamon with white cheese.

Drinks

Beer, often locally brewed, tastes good and is reasonably priced. Imported wines and spirits are available but expensive. In the Netherlands Antilles, all the famous Dutch beers are available, as well as Amstel, brewed on Curaçao. It's the world's only beer made from distilled seawater.

The light, aromatic rum of the Caribbean, white or dark, is rightly famous, and forms the base of many cocktails and punches. *Ti punch*, Creole for *petit punch*, is just that, three or four measures of white rum to one of sugar cane syrup and a dash of lime. Though most common as an apéritif, punch is also the local early-morning pick-me-up, the late-night cordial and the

most frequent drink with a meal. The popular *piña colada* consists of rum, coconut cream, crushed pineapple (or juice) and crushed ice. Most bartenders have their own personal recipe for planter's punch: a refreshing concoction of lime juice, sugar syrup and crushed ice, with a sprinkling of nutmeg or bitters. Rum daiquiris come in many flavours, including coconut, banana, guava, soursop, peach and strawberry.

A non-alcoholic favourite is coconut water fresh from the shell cleanly beheaded with one swipe of a machete.

If you get the chance, try some *mauby*, a popular cooling beverage made from roots and bark, with heavy lacings of cinnamon, clove and other herbs and spices.

Curaçao is the home of the famed orange liqueur, distilled from a secret recipe and bottled in several colours and flavours. Aruba's very own liqueur, *cuicui*, is made from the leaves of the aloe plant. Red and liquorice-flavoured, it dates back to the times of the Arawak Indians. Saba produces a liqueur based on rum and known as Saba Spice.

The world's best coffee comes from Jamaica's Blue Mountains.

Flavours of the Caribbean: exotic fruit, chicken soup, fried red snapper and a drink in a coconut.

Corbis/Kaehler

istockphoto.com/Seth

istockphoto.com/Sanchez

istockphoto.com/Zhou

HORS-D

RHUM VIEU

Distillerie Bie

Take home a bottle of rum—they say it's a
good remedy for rheumatism.

Huber/Dutton

SHOPPING

There are two shopping categories in the Caribbean—local handicrafts and imported duty-free articles. People flock to places such as St Thomas in the Virgin Islands where tax-free shopping is big business. Even "I Hate Shopping" types succumb to the fever of spending. This is retail therapy at its most addictive.

Island Crafts

The arts and crafts scene is alive and well, with numerous galleries selling paintings, sculpture and pottery by local artists. Hunt around the markets for colourful and unusual souvenirs: sensational beachwear in bright batik patterns; woodcarvings; hand-embroidered and crocheted mats and tablecloths in spidery lace designs. The old sailor's craft of macramé still flourishes on the islands, appearing in wall-hangings, plant-holders and so on. Scrimshaw, an 18th-century fisherman's hobby, is still alive in some places. Choose from pendants and buckles of shell or bone engraved with nautical scenes.

There's no lack in imaginative jewellery, but beware of items made from shells or coral as they may be confiscated at customs.

Gourmet gifts include homemade jams and jellies in exotic flavours—tamarind, sea grape, papaya pickle, genip, hibiscus— or bottled pepper sauce. There are West Indian spices and seasonings and bush tea—herbs and leaves the natives use for a brisk, possibly therapeutic infusion. Light and dark rums have been a speciality of the islands for three centuries and are a bargain.

Island perfumes and cosmetics make use of indigenous ingredients. Lavish amounts of the precious gel from the Caribbean plant aloe vera are used in products for skin and hair, as well as coconut oil and paba gel in tanning lotions, sun blocks and lip balms.

Don't forget a straw or sisal sunhat and beachmat, and a large wicker basket to carry all your purchases home.

Local Colour

No doubt you'll also want to buy something typical of your particular island. Some favourites:

ABC Islands
Spirits and liqueurs (especially curaçao) and spices. Bonaire: T-shirts and tea-towels decorated with the flamingo motif.

Anguilla
At The Valley post office, you'll find attractive postage stamps and commemorative issues, such as the Caribbean Fishes series, the Fruits of Anguilla, ancient Anguillan sailing vessels, the island hotels, or goats.

Antigua
A warri board—the Antiguan equivalent of backgammon, which some say is as challenging as chess; red clay pottery; clay charcoal pots for grilling fish and meat.

Barbados
Locally distilled rum, said to be the best of all.

Cayman Islands
Jewellery fashioned from local semi-precious stones such as caymanite, veined with shades of orange, brown, cream and black; numismatic jewellery crafted from old coins retrieved from sunken vessels, mounted in exquisite gold and diamond settings. Do not buy items of black coral or turtle shell: they will be confiscated by customs officials when you return home.

Dominica
The Caribs make reed baskets interwoven with banana leaves and carve small souvenirs in wood. Look for hats and bags of vetiver grass, place mats and souvenirs made from bamboo or coconut. The Dominicans also make pretty straw mats called *khus-khus* with geometric patterns, flower or fish motifs.

French Antilles
Dolls in Creole madras costume; an inflated spiny puffer fish *(poisson-hérisson)* which can become an off-beat lampshade if large enough; gold hoop earrings called *créoles*; lengths of madras fabric; local rum—bay rum distilled in Les Saintes is renowned as a remedy for rheumatism. And luxury goods imported from France, sold at prices even cheaper than "duty-free" islands: cosmetics and perfumes, designer fashions, porcelain, crystal, wines and liqueurs.

Grenada
Baskets woven of straw or palm fronds, filled with ginger, cinnamon, nutmeg and other spices.

Jamaica
A Rastafarian beret with a fringe of false dreadlocks attached; Rastafarian carvings on lignum vitae, a light-coloured hardwood; a recording of reggae or calypso music; reproductions of pewter

and china from the submerged city of Port Royal; a bottle of rum, Rumona (rum liqueur) or Tia Maria (coffee and chocolate liqueur); pepper jellies; Blue Mountain coffee.

Montserrat
Souvenirs of the volcano: postcards, T-shirts and carvings made from volcanic rocks and ash.

Puerto Rico
Hand-carved wooden figures of saints, *santos*; straw hats, such as the *pava*, an upswept model worn by farmers *en la isla*, full-sized or miniature; *guayaberas*, tailored, fancily embroidered shirts worn by Puerto Rican gentlemen; hand-rolled cigars.

Saba
A bottle or two of Saba Spice; fine linen featuring the intricate drawn-thread needlework known as Saba lace, or Spanish work, introduced from South America more than a century ago.

Statia
Traditional woodwork; silk-screen printing on cotton; water-colours of island scenes.

Long-lasting souvenirs: the much-prized Blue Mountain coffee; spices for your kitchen; paintings by local artists; sunset-coloured fabrics.

hemis.fr/Du Boisberranger

hemis.fr/Du Boisberranger

JPM Guides

hemis.fr/Gardel

St Lucia
Tropical flowers shipped fresh from the island's fields to your home by courier. Or carry their fragrance home yourself in the form of locally blended perfume.

St Kitts and Nevis
Beautiful postage stamps; Nevis cooking pots made of red clay.

St Vincent and the Grenadines
Sea Island cotton clothes; costumed dolls in ruffled dresses; mahogany carvings; postage stamps; green palm-frond sunhats woven for you while you wait.

Trinidad
Indian silks, cotton shirts and caftans; typical loose shirts bought for a song at street stalls; silver and gold filigree Indian-style jewellery; tapes or CDs of pan and calypso music; or a steel pan to play it yourself.

Turks and Caicos
Rare conch pearls.

Virgin Islands
Mocko jumbie dolls, from the heart of native folklore, come dressed as a clown.

Duty-Free
Luxury goods from all over the world are available at considerably reduced prices in Aruba, the Cayman Islands, Curaçao and the other Netherlands Antilles, Grenada, Jamaica, St Lucia, St Martin and the Virgin Islands. You may need proof of your visitor's status when you make purchases. Some islands have special regulations: in Jamaica, alcohol and tobacco are delivered to your point of departure, but you can carry away "in-bond" purchases, which can only be opened out of Jamaican waters. In Barbados, you can obtain duty-free goods at any time during your stay, with the exception of tobacco, alcohol and electronic goods, which must be bought at the airport just before you leave the island.

The Virgin Islands are particular favourites with American shoppers, as they can take home up to $1,600 worth of duty-free goods. Charlotte Amalie on St Thomas is the biggest centre, where the most varied and luxurious goods are found on or near Main Street. Delivery is well organized and efficient; goods can be taken immediately to your ship or plane, or expertly dispatched to your home address. Items on sale range from English cashmere to Thai silks, from Danish silver to Japanese cameras, from Portuguese embroidery to Swiss watches and knives. And all manner of gemstones, including a local stone, larimar, its colour varying from light blue to deep blue-green.

General editor
Barbara Ender

Concept
Karin Palazzolo

Layout
Luc Malherbe
Matias Jolliet

Photo credits
p. 1 hemis.fr/Gardel
p. 2: istockphoto.com/Perales
(shell); /jmproductions (fins);
/Young (steel drums);
/rgomezphoto (boat)

Maps
JPM Publications

Copyright ©2010, 2003
JPM Publications S.A.
12, avenue William-Fraisse,
1006 Lausanne, Switzerland
information@jpmguides.com
http://www.jpmguides.com/

All rights reserved. No part
of this book may be reproduced
or transmitted in any form or
by any means, electronic or
mechanical, including
photocopying, recording or
by any information storage
and retrieval system without
permission in writing from the
publisher.

Every care has been taken to
verify the information in the
guide, but the publisher cannot
accept responsibility for any
errors that may have occurred.
If you spot an inaccuracy or a
serious omission, please let
us know.

Printed in Switzerland
12690.00.6775
Swissprinters IRL, Lausanne
Edition 2010